9-11-68

COLLECTED POEMS

1967

COLLECTED POEMS
1967

ELIZABETH JENNINGS

DUFOUR EDITIONS
1967

Library of Congress catalog card no. 67-27373

PRINTED IN GREAT BRITAIN BY
NORTHUMBERLAND PRESS LIMITED
GATESHEAD

For Hildebrand James, O.P.

CONTENTS

A SENSE OF THE WORLD, 1958

RECOVERIES, 1964

THE MIND HAS MOUNTAINS, 1966

THE SONNETS OF MICHELANGELO, 1961

NEW POEMS

ACKNOWLEDGEMENTS

Poems (1953) was first published by The Fantasy Press; *The Sonnets of Michelangelo* (1961) was first published by the Folio Society; *A Way of Looking* (1955), *A Sense of the World* (1958), *Song for a Birth or a Death* (1961), and *Recoveries* (1964) were first published by André Deutsch. The author wishes to acknowledge the kindness of these publishers in permitting her to reprint here some of the poems from those books.

POEMS

1953

DELAY

The radiance of that star that leans on me
Was shining years ago. The light that now
Glitters up there my eye may never see,
And so the time lag teases me with how

Love that loves now may not reach me until
Its first desire is spent. The star's impulse
Must wait for eyes to claim it beautiful
And love arrived may find us somewhere else.

WINTER LOVE

Let us have winter loving that the heart
May be in peace and ready to partake
Of the slow pleasure spring would wish to hurry
Or that in summer harshly would awake,
And let us fall apart, O gladly weary,
The white skin shaken like a white snowflake.

WEATHERCOCK

A hard tin bird was my lover
Fluttering with every breeze
To north and west would hover
In fierce extremities
But I would never find
Him quietly in the south
Or in the warmest east
And never near my mouth
And never on my breast.

A hard bird swinging high
Glinting with gold and sun
Aloft swung in the sky
Ready to run
O would I were that sun
He swings to with desire
Could see my love's gold eye
And feel his fire.

THE SUBSTITUTE

He rehearsed then with an understudy
(Love he had cast not ready to play the part
Nor knowing yet disturbance in the heart).
Nearly indifferent he explored the body
Of one untutored, ready to be hurt,
Absolute, being unpractised in the role.

She took the lesson wholly in the school
Of his rehearsal, learnt it thoroughly,
Played it entire while his mind still was full
Of the other with whom he could not be,
Who played a passion quite away from him.

If she his waking love and she his dream
Used cruelly should meet, his love would stir
A sympathy and union in them,
The loved and loving have a common theme,
And he the instigator be in neither
But as the cause they recognised each other.

SEQUENCE FROM CHILDHOOD

I

Children ponder our possessions with
Minds that are free, they play with curious fears.
Adept at suffering second-hand, their legends
Are dire with cruelty. As overseers
They watch with fascination from the path.

Their truth being other than the facts, their brigands,
Pirates and thieves can be shut up at night,
But move like mice within their dreams beneath
The floor of sleep and with the morning light
Appear, unlike ours, fabulous as death.

ADOPTED CHILD

'This' they say 'Is what we could not have.
How strange for other lovers to impart
A meeting thus. And separate from the love
Barren between us, this child grows to move
Almost against the turning of our heart.'

'Our failure thus shall walk about our son,
Learn to speak dutifully to his parents
Who know him their escape, whose love moves on
To gesture at so tender a pretence
And make a home in others' innocence.'

But love is inward still, however they
Walk in the child and make him weather all
The tenderness that neither could fulfil,
And never 'This is you' will either say
Passing a passion to the child to seal
Their lack, but watch a stranger ignorantly.

TIME

Why should we think of ends, beginnings
Who for a moment draw our pace
Through moons and sunsets, risings, wanings,
Who brush the moment, seek a place
More than a minute's hopes and winnings?

Why cannot we accept the hour,
The present, be observers and
Hold a full knowledge in our power,
Arrest the falling of the sand,
And keep the watchful moment, pour
Its meaning in the hurried hand?

REMINISCENCE

When I was happy alone, too young for love
Or to be loved in any but a way
Cloudless and gentle, I would find the day
Long as I wished its length or web to weave.

I did not know or could not know enough
To fret at thought or even try to whittle
A pattern from the shapeless stony stuff
That now confuses since I've grown too subtle.

I used the senses, did not seek to find
Something they could not touch, made numb with fear;
I felt the glittering landscape in the mind
And O was happy not to have it clear.

FANTASY

Tree without a leaf I stand
Bird unfeathered cannot fly
I a beggar weep and cry
Not for coins but for a hand

To beg with. All my leaves are down
Feathers flown and hand wrenched off
Bird and tree and beggar grown
Nothing on account of love.

ITALIAN LIGHT

It is not quite a house without the sun
And sun is what we notice, wonder at
As if stone left its hard and quarried state
To be reciprocal to light and let
The falling beams bound and rebound upon
Shutter and wall, each with assurance thrown.

So on descending from the snow we meet
Not warmth of south but houses which contrive
To be designed of sun. The builders have
Instructed hands to know where shadows fall
And made of buildings an obedient stone
Linked to the sun as waters to the moon.

AFTERNOON IN FLORENCE

This afternoon disturbs within the mind
No other afternoon, is out of time
Yet lies within a definite sun to end
In night that is in time. Yet hold it here
Our eyes, our minds, to make the city clear.

Light detains no prisoner here at all
In brick or stone but sends a freedom out
Extends a shadow like a deeper thought,
Makes churches move, once still,
Rocking in light as music rocks the bell.

So eyes make room for light and
minds make room
For image of the city tangible.
We look down on the city and a dream
Opens to wakefulness, and waking on
This peace perpetuates this afternoon.

THE PLANNERS

Some who fell in love with lack of order
And liked the random weather, were made angry,
Accused the planners thus 'It is not brick
Only you set upright and scaffolding
And the roof bending at a perfect angle,
But all our love you end in measurements,
Construct a mood for any moment, teach
Passion to move in inches not by chance'.

And swarming from the forests to new houses
They chipped the walls a little, left footmarks
Across the thresholds, would not scan each other
By clock or compass, terrified the silence
With rough words that had never been thought out.

And builders, poets fell upon them, saw
A just disorder for their alteration,
Would turn the conversation into music,
Tidy the house and from the lovers' quarrel
Shape a whole scene with middle, end, beginning,
Never be wearied of the straightening out
Though would not recognise they fell in love
Most deeply at the centre of disaster.

THE HARBOUR

No ship is stationed here for greatness, white
Sails urge forward only momentary
Prowess and funnels strike brief attitudes.
Each cargo lifted out is commentary
On all small voyages, all seaward loss,
No sunburn on a sailor what it was.

Mere idleness is proud, is a lifted thought.
(Here leaning upon a bollard or tapping a pipe
On a boat's steep side means 'I am entirely myself')
All ships but shuffle through the harbour, bells
Suggest that tides are seeking something else,
And only cargo at a looked-for end
Is rich for promise or a giving hand.

So this is not the place to ask a tragic
Meaning, a gesture that decides a pause
In ordinariness. Movement is loss,
Yet sailors draw up anchors from their peace
And all pass forward to a wave's rough logic.
Even the watchful one upon the wharf
Is less himself because the ships must hurry
Relative always, hindrances to love.

THE ARRIVAL

See how travel conveys him as love can
Out of himself. This is not I I feel,
He thinks, but sets himself in will
New-made to stare, to take a virtue out,
And wonders how to meet all those who fill
The jetty there and wonders how they wait

For him who does not know himself at all;
And though his movement states 'I am'
He argues with his own identity,
Sees, somewhere back, himself at sea,
Him starting out, him, further still, at home,
And wonders which to gather up to greet
Those waiting who are nothing but
their thought
Of strangeness and another way to meet.

THE STRANGER

This stranger looks for no encouragement,
Concerns himself with silence, ceases movement
To learn a landscape, yes to grow in it,
And trade all old familiar settings for
The slightest cypress, or one shuttered villa,
A sharp incline, so long as not familiar.

And finds this loss of past a gain to him,
Confronts another's eyes and finds a candour
A warmer look as if he took it from
A recent love-making, and this is love—
To find new roots strike in this country deep
And feel a friendship like wind through
the landscape.

IDENTITY

When I decide I shall assemble you
Or, more precisely, when I decide which thoughts
Of mine about you fit most easily together,
Then I can learn what I have loved, what lets
Light through the mind. The residue
Of what you may be goes. I gather

Only as lovers or friends gather at all
For making friends means this—
Image and passion combined into a whole
Pattern within the loving mind, not her or his
Concurring there. You can project the full
Picture of lover or friend that is not either.

So then assemble me,
Your exact picture firm and credible,
Though as I think myself I may be free
And accurate enough.
That you love what is truthful to your will
Is all that ever can be answered for
And, what is more,
Is all we make each other when we love.

THE SETTLERS

A land once questioned only by the sea
Which carried pebbles off as property,
And spoken to by bird or animal
Or a weight of wind trespassing a little,
But now the water throws explorers up
Whose eyes possess and hearts begin to settle.

Climate becomes a privilege for them
Offered to later visitors like love,
And all the corn cut down and packed away
Loses the sun a little and casts off
The lash of wind. The complete natural kingdom
Is tamed and ruled, even the sea discouraged.

And the rebellion of an earthquake shaking
The crops awry, throwing the houses down,
Killing a few, finds only the next morning
Bruised dreamers planning and the workmen taking
The broken bricks to build another town.

And men who come to meditate a mountain
Are tamed too by the dwellers here and offered
Weather for happiness, children to show
The white church in the market-place, the fountain
That mocks the uncouth sea. They go away
Ignorant that they alone are undiscovered.

THE IDLER

An idler holds that rose as always rose,
Will not, before the bud discloses it
Within a later season, in his thought
Unwrap the flower and force the petals open
And wish in mind a different rose to happen.

So will not colour it with his own shadow
As we contrive, living beyond the present,
To move all things away from their
own moment
And state another time for us. O who
Watches may yet make time refuse to grow.

So has his subtle power wiser than ours
And need elaborate no peace at all.
Watch how a landscape kindest is to idlers
Helping their shiftlessness grow to new powers,
Composing stillness round their careless will.

BELL-RINGER

The bells renew the town, discover it
And give it back itself again, the man
Pulling the rope collects the houses as
Thoughts gather in the mind unscanned, he is
Crowding the town together from the night
And making bells the morning, in remote

Control of every life (for bells shout 'Wake'
And shake out dreams, though it is he who pulls
The sleep aside). But not into his thought
Do men continue as in lives of power;

For when each bell is pulled sufficiently
He never sees himself as any cause
Or need; the sounds had left his hands to sing
A meaning for each listening separately,
A separate meaning for the single choice.

Yet bells retire to silence, need him when
Time must be shown a lucid interval
And men look up as if the air were full
Of birds descending, bells exclaiming in
His hands but shouting wider than his will.

THE CLIMBERS

To the cold peak without their careful women
(Who watching children climbing into dreams
Go dispossessed at home). The mountain moves
Away at every climb and steps are hard
Frozen along the glacier. Every man
Tied to the rope constructs himself alone.

And not the summit reached nor any pole
Touched is the wished embrace, but still to move
And as the mountain climbs to see it whole
And each mind's landscape growing more complete
As sinews strain and all the muscles knot.

One at the peak is small. His disappointment
The coloured flag flown at the lonely top,
And all the valley's motive grown obscure.
He envies the large toilers halfway there
Who still possess the mountain by desire
And, not arriving, dream in no resentment.

FISHERMEN

This to be peace, they think beside the river
Being adapted well to expectation
And their wives' mutiny at no achievement,
And yet can sit watching the promises
Escape through weeds and make a trial of biting,
Can lose them, thankful that it is not yet
Time to draw in the line and drain the net.

Learning themselves in this uncertainty
Each hardly cares whether a fish is caught,
For here is privacy, each warns himself,
The fish, inquiries in the river, not
When drawn out promises at all
Being so solid on the bank and still.

Only the boys who live in certainty,
With expectation other than the stream,
Jeer at the patience and draw up their net
Of future frogs, the river vague to them
Until it's emptied. But the old men fill
Their eyes with water, leave the river full.

THE ISLAND

All travellers escape the mainland here.
The same geology torn from the stretch
Of hostile homelands is a head of calm,
And the same sea that pounds a foreign beach
Turns strangers here familiar, looses them
Kindly as pebbles shuffled up the shore.

Each brings an island in his heart to square
With what he finds, and all is something strange
But most expected. In this innocent air
Thoughts can assume a meaning, island strength
Is outward, inward, each man measures it,
Unrolls his happiness a shining length.

And this awareness grows upon itself,
Fastens on minds, is forward, backward, here.
The island focuses escape and free
Men on the shore are also islands, steer
Self to knowledge of self in the calm sea,
Seekers who are their own discovery.

A WAY OF LOOKING

1955

POEM IN WINTER

Today the children begin to hope for snow
And look in the sky for auguries of it.
It is not for such omens that we wait,
Our world may not be settled by the slow
Falling of flakes to lie across our thought.

And even if the snow comes down indeed
We still shall stand behind a pane of glass
Untouched by it, and watch the children press
Their image on the drifts the snow has laid
Upon a winter they think they have made.

This is a wise illusion. Better to
Believe the near world is created by
A wish, a shaping hand, a certain eye,
Than hide in the mind's corner as we do
As though there were no world, no fall of snow.

SONG AT THE BEGINNING OF AUTUMN

Now watch this autumn that arrives
In smells. All looks like summer still;
Colours are quite unchanged, the air
On green and white serenely thrives.
Heavy the trees with growth and full
The fields. Flowers flourish everywhere.

Proust who collected time within
A child's cake would understand
The ambiguity of this—
Summer still raging while a thin
Column of smoke stirs from the land
Proving that autumn gropes for us.

But every season is a kind
Of rich nostalgia. We give names—
Autumn and summer, winter, spring—
As though to unfasten from the mind
Our moods and give them outward forms.
We want the certain, solid thing.

But I am carried back against
My will into a childhood where
Autumn is bonfires, marbles, smoke;
I lean against my window fenced
From evocations in the air.
When I said autumn, autumn broke.

KINGS

You send an image hurrying out of doors
When you depose a king and seize his throne:
You exile symbols when you take by force.

And even if you say the power's your own,
That you are your own hero, your own king
You will not wear the meaning of the crown.

The power a ruler has is how men bring
Their thoughts to bear upon him, how their minds
Construct the grandeur from the simple thing.

And kings prevented from their proper ends
Make a deep lack in men's imagining;
Heroes are nothing without worshipping,

Will not diminish into lovers, friends.

THE ENEMIES

Last night they came across the river and
Entered the city. Women were awake
With lights and food. They entertained the band,
Not asking what the men had come to take
Or what strange tongue they spoke
Or why they came so suddenly through the land.

Now in the morning all the town is filled
With stories of the swift and dark invasion;
The women say that not one stranger told
A reason for his coming. The intrusion
Was not for devastation:
Peace is apparent still on hearth and field.

Yet all the city is a haunted place.
Man meeting man speaks cautiously. Old friends
Close up the candid looks upon their face.
There is no warmth in hands accepting hands;
Each ponders, 'Better hide myself in case
Those strangers have set up their homes in minds
I used to walk in. Better draw the blinds
Even if the strangers haunt in my own house.'

IN THIS TIME

If the myth's outworn, the legend broken,
  Useless even within the child's story
Since he sees well they now bring lights no longer
  Into our eyes: and if our past retreats
And blows away like dust along the desert,
  Not leading to our moment now at all,
Settling us in this place and saying 'Here
  In you I shall continue'—then what kind
Of lives have we? Can we make myths revive
  By breathing on them? Is there any taper
That will return the glitter to our eyes?

We have retreated inwards to our minds
  Too much, have made rooms there with all doors closed,
All windows shuttered. There we sit and mope
  The myth away, set by the lovely legends;
Hardly we hear the children shout outside.
  We only know a way to love ourselves,
Have lost the power that made us lose ourselves.
  O let the wind outside blow in again
And the dust come and all the children's voices.
  Let anything that is not us return.
Myths are the memories we have rejected
  And legends need the freedom of our minds.

THE LOST SYMBOLS

Missing the symbol they restore the fact:
How seven years back this city was burned down
And minds were gutted too. Men learnt to act
As though there were no meaning in the town,
And chose at last to make as derelict
All dreams they fostered. Dreams are also one
With walls and roofs and they like ashes lie
When a fired city cries for elegy.

Soon stone was piled on stone, another city
Replaced the ruin with its shadow and
Men walked in it but knew it had a beauty
Not like the one that burnt beneath their hand.
The dreams would not return. Men's minds were weighty
With all the sense of searching for a land
Revealing symbols that a man might hold
Within the heart and from those symbols build.

It is the fine tradition they have lost
That spoke in architectural styles, that rang
Out with the bells when all the bells were tossed
And voices spoke up in the sounds and sang,
And men put feet down firmly in the dust
That flowered a legend and the legend was
Their way of life and a man's peaceful cause.

Now they assemble all the facts to learn
New symbols. For their minds are so constructed
That every fact they must to image turn
And dream new dreams when towns are resurrected.
The meaning is not clear — the burning down
And the charred minds. They would have all collected
In visions to be lived. The only style,
The only symbol is in each one's will.

BEYOND POSSESSION

Our images withdraw, the rose returns
To what it was before we looked at it.
We lift our look from where the water runs
And it's pure river once again, we write
No emblems on the trees. A way begins
Of living where we have no need to beat
The petals down to get the scent of rose
Or sign our features where the water goes.

All is itself. Each man himself entire,
Not even plucking out his thought, not even
Bringing a tutored wilfulness to bear
Upon the rose, the water. Each has given
Essence of water back to itself, essence of flower,
Till he is yoked to his own heart and driven
Inward to find a private kind of peace
And not a mind reflecting his own face.

Yet must go deeper still, must move to love
Where thought is free to let the water ride,
Is liberal to the rose giving it life
And setting even its own shadow aside;
Till flower and water blend with freedom of
Passion that does not close them in and hide
Their deepest natures; but the heart is strong
To beat with rose and river in one song.

ON MAKING

All you who build, whether the marvellous columns
  Or the splendid stanza echoing itself,
Is there a place for you to stand and watch
  And truthfully swear 'My part in this is finished'
With a mind quite empty of its images
  That fit best in another kind of freedom?

There is no place at all. Your satisfaction
  Fails with the last brick laid, with the final word.
There is no place for minds to stand at ease
  Nor any mood where passion may partake
Of stillness and be still. Move on, move out
  Riding your mind with reckless animation.

Look there are men living within your houses
  Look there are minds moving through your poems,
Proving how much you left unmade, unsaid.
  Your work is done yet there is no completion.
Only when inspiration is lived along
  Dare you exclaim 'I'm near the perfect thing
That is not mine nor what I made at all.'

TRIBUTE

Sometimes the tall poem leans across the page
And the whole world seems near, a simple thing.
Then all the arts of mind and hand engage
To make the shadow tangible. O white
As silence is the page where words shall sing
And all the shadows be drawn into light.

And no one else is necessary then.
The poem is enough that joins me to
The world that seems too far to grasp at when
Images fail and words are gabbled speech:
At those times clarity appears in you,
Your mind holds meanings that my mind can reach.

Are you remote, then, when words play their part
With a fine arrogance within the poem?
Will the words keep all else outside my heart,
Even you, my test of life and gauge?
No, for you are that place where poems find room,
The tall abundant shadow on my page.

FOR A CHILD BORN DEAD

What ceremony can we fit
You into now? If you had come
Out of a warm and noisy room
To this, there'd be an opposite
For us to know you by. We could
Imagine you in lively mood

And then look at the other side,
The mood drawn out of you, the breath
Defeated by the power of death.
But we have never seen you stride
Ambitiously the world we know.
You could not come and yet you go.

But there is nothing now to mar
Your clear refusal of our world.
Not in our memories can we mould
You or distort your character.
Then all our consolation is
That grief can be as pure as this.

COMMUNICATION

No use to speak, no good to tell you that
A love is worn away not by the one
Who leaves but by the one who stays and hopes,
Since you would rather have the hoping still
Than be yourself again. What can I say
Who know, better than you, the one who has
Moved on, away, not loving him at all?

And certainly to you I would relinquish
This knowledge held in other ways of feeling
Though dressed up in the properties of passion
Looked at by you. Something is deeply held
By me who never deeply searched at all
And we are not yet wise enough or subtle
To offer anyone a state of mind.

This the particular problem, and I search
A power over our general condition,
Where love is like a landscape we can change
And where desire may be transformed to friendship
If friendship gives the really wanted knowledge,
Where we can see the end and have the power
To take the journey there a different way,
And we can move our minds as we move houses:
Where love is more than lucky in the land.

MIRRORS

Was it a mirror then across a room,
A crowded room of parties where the smoke
Rose to the ceiling with the talk? The glass
Stared back at me a half-familiar face
Yet something hoped for. When at last you came
It was as if the distant mirror spoke.

That loving ended as all self-love ends
And teaches us that only fair-grounds have
The right to show us halls of mirrors where
In every place we look we see our stare
Taunting our own identies. But love
Perceives without a mirror in the hands.

IN THE NIGHT

Out of my window late at night I gape
And see the stars but do not watch them really,
And hear the trains but do not listen clearly;
Inside my mind I turn about to keep
Myself awake, yet am not there entirely.
Something of me is out in the dark landscape.

How much am I then what I think, how much what I feel?
How much the eye that seems to keep stars straight?
Do I control what I can contemplate
Or is it my vision that's amenable?
I turn in my mind, my mind is a room whose wall
I can see the top of but never completely scale.

All that I love is, like the night, outside,
Good to be gazed at, looking as if it could
With a simple gesture be brought inside my head
Or in my heart. But my thoughts about it divide
Me from my object. Now deep in my bed
I turn and the world turns on the other side.

RECAPITULATION

Being a child it was enough to stand
  The centre of a world and let success
Come crowding in, be taken by the hand.
This was one way to lose a loneliness.

Until success itself became a part
  I played. It was the shell and centre too.
My mind was somewhere else, also my heart.
  I could not tell the false self from the true.

Now I abandon all my attributes —
  Failure, success, despair — until I have
Nothing at all but hard invincible doubts
  Shaping the one self that I can believe.

ANSWERS

I kept my answers small and kept them near;
Big questions bruised my mind but still I let
Small answers be a bulwark to my fear.

The huge abstractions I kept from the light;
Small things I handled and caressed and loved.
I let the stars assume the whole of night.

But the big answers clamoured to be moved
Into my life. Their great audacity
Shouted to be acknowledged and believed.

Even when all small answers build up to
Protection of my spirit, still I hear
Big answers striving for their overthrow

And all the great conclusions coming near.

A SENSE OF THE WORLD

1958

'It becometh you to retain a glorious sense of the world.'

THOMAS TRAHERNE

THE CHILD AND THE SHADOW

Your shadow I have seen you play with often.
O and it seems a shadow light before you,
Glittering behind you. You can see what lies
Beneath its marking dappled on the water
    Or on the earth a footprint merely;
No total darkness is cast by your body.

Say that it is a game of identities this—
You chasing yourself not caring whatever you find.
You have not sought a use for mirrors yet,
It is not your own shadow that you watch,
    Only our world which you learn slowly:
Our shadows strive to mingle with your own,

Chase them, then, as you chase the leaves or a bird,
Disturb us, disturb us, still let the light lie gently
Under the place that you carve for yourself in air;
Look, the fish are darting beneath your reflection
    But you see deep beyond your glance:
It is our shadow that slides in between.

OLD WOMAN

So much she caused she cannot now account for
As she stands watching day return, the cool
Walls of the house moving towards the sun.
She puts some flowers in a vase and thinks
'There is not much I can arrange
In here and now, but flowers are suppliant

As children never were. And love is now
A flicker of memory, my body is
My own entirely. When I lie at night
I gather nothing now into my arms,
No child or man, and where I live
Is what remains when men and children go.'

Yet she owns more than residue of lives
That she has marked and altered. See how she
Warns time from too much touching her possessions
By keeping flowers fed, by polishing
Her fine old silver. Gratefully
She sees her own glance printed on grandchildren.

Drawing the curtains back and opening windows
Every morning now, she feels her years
Grow less and less. Time puts no burden on
Her now she does not need to measure it.
It is acceptance she arranges
And her own life she places in the vase.

OLD MAN

His age drawn out behind him to be watched:
It is his shadow you may say. That dark
He paints upon the wall is his past self,
A mark he only leaves when he is still
    And he is still now always,
At ease and watching all his life assemble.

And he intends nothing but watching. What
His life has made of him his shadow shows—
Fine graces gone but dignity remaining,
While all he shuffled after is composed
    Into a curve of dark, of silences:
An old man tranquil in his silences.

And we move round him, are his own world turning,
Spinning it seems to him, leaving no shadow
To blaze our trail. We are our actions only:
He is himself, abundant and assured,
    All action thrown away,
And time is slowing where his shadow stands.

THE CHILD AND THE SEASHELL

Never the certainty of it now but only
Far-off forebodings, tides tending to silence,
The lip of the sea usurping the shell not shore,
And this is the lip he puts to his ear and listens,
Listens and waits for the far-off hum, the drowning,
    The sliding and suck of shingle
As if an echo were lifted off the surface

Of water, as if the sea, withdrawn for long,
Left only the sound of itself and this he hears
Dim in the corridors of the twisted shell;
For him now, more than the real sea, this is
Promise and expectation of worlds where he
    Might possibly sail. The shell,
Sleeping in its own silence, admits all seas.

And the child, still in the mood for every promise
Rewarding him, listens to great commotions,
To storms abating, to men dragging on driftwood,
And does not know that never will sea so sound,
That shores which wait for his footprints now will never
    So slip like a shadow beneath
His mind, as this shell now in perfect silence
Steeps his whole being in seas now forever nameless.

TAKEN BY SURPRISE

Before, the anticipation, the walk merely
Under the oaks, (the afternoon crushed down
To his pressed footprints), noon surrendered, forgotten—
And the man moving, singular under the sun
With the hazel held in his hand lightly, lightly:
On the edge of his ear the lisp of the wind among
Untrembling leaves. Sun at the tips of the trees
Looked down, looked cold, and the man felt easy there.
His shadow seemed fitting as never before it was,
And the almost silence a space a man may enter
And be forgotten by all but his secret thoughts.
Then, something taking his fingers: 'Is it the wind?'
He thought and looked to see if the branches moved.
But nothing unusual stirred the trees, again
His fingers trembled, the hazel shook, he felt
Suddenly life in the twig as a woman feels
Abrupt and close the stir of the unborn child.
O and the afternoon was altered then;
Power from all quarters flung at him, silence broke
And deft but uneasy far in the back of his mind
A word like water shuddered, streams gushed and fountains
Rose as the hazel leapt from his mastered hand.

THE STORM

Right in the middle of the storm it was.
So many winds were blowing none could tell
Which was the fiercest or if trees that bent
So smoothly to each impulse had been waiting
All of their growing-time for just that impulse
To prove how pliable they were. Beneath,
Beasts fled away through fern, and stiffest grasses,
Which bent like fluid things, made tidal motion.

These who had never met before but in
Calmest surroundings, found all shadows mingling;
No stance could be struck here, no peace attained,
And words blew round in broken syllables,
Half-meanings sounded out like trumpet blasts,
Decisive words were driven into hiding.
Yet some hilarity united them
And faces, carved and cleared by rain and lightning,
Stared out as if they never had been seen.

And children now, lost in the wood together,
Becoming the behaviour of the wind,
The way the light fell, learnt each other newly
And sudden gentleness was apprehended
Till the abating winds, the whole storm swerving
Into another quarter, left them standing
Unwild and watching in bewilderment
Their own delusive shadows slow and part.

HER GARDEN

Not at the full noon will she pick those flowers
For sudden shade indoors would make them wilt.
The petals would drop down on polished wood
Adding another element to decay
Which all her old rooms are infected with.

Only outside she can put off the course
Of her disease. She has the garden built
Within high walls so no one can intrude.
When people pass she only hears the way
Their footsteps sound, never their closer breath.

But in her borders she observes the powers
Of bud and branch, forgetting how she felt
When, blood within her veins like sap, she stood,
Her arms like branches bare above the day
And all the petals strewn along her path.

No matter now for she has bridged the pause
Between fruition and decay. She'll halt
A little in her garden while a mood
Of peace so fills her that she cannot say
Whether it is the flowers' life or her death.

SUMMER AND TIME

Now when the days descend
We do not let them lie
But ponder on the end,
How morning air drained dry
Of mist will but contend
Later with evening sky.

And so we mix up time.
Children, we say, ignore
Before and after, chime
Only the present hour.
But we are wrong, they climb
What time is aiming for

But beg no lastingness.
And it is we who try
In every hour to press
Befores and afters, sigh
All the great hour's success
And set the spoiling by.

Heavy the heat today,
Even the clocks seem slow.
But children make no play
With summers years ago.
It is we who betray
Who tease the sun-dial so.

AT NOON

Lying upon my bed I see
Full noon at ease. Each way I look
A world established without me
Proclaims itself. I take a book
And flutter through the pages where
Sun leaps through shadows. And I stare

Straight through the words and find again
A world that has no need of me.
The poems stride against the strain
Of complex rhythms. Separately
I lie and struggle to become
More than a centre to this room.

I want the ease of noon outside
Also the strength of words which move
Against their music. All the wide
And casual day I need to stuff
With my own meaning and the book
Of poems reflect me where I look.

THE DANCERS

See how they move with strange smooth faces now.
Their feet find sympathy they never found
In words, their joy is bouncing on the ground.
The faster that they move the more they show
Soft and impassive features. It's as though

Thought were abandoned and the mind grown small,
And we sense peace however fast they move.
Some centre they have found, silent and still
Round which they dance. It looks like love until
The music stops, they separate and send
Shudders of some betrayal through us all.

GHOSTS

Those houses haunt in which we leave
Something undone. It is not those
Great words or silences of love

That spread their echoes through a place
And fill the locked-up unbreathed gloom.
Ghosts do not haunt with any face

That we have known; they only come
With arrogance to thrust at us
Our own omissions in a room.

The words we would not speak they use,
The deeds we dared not act they flaunt,
Our nervous silences they bruise;

It is our helplessness they choose
And our refusals that they haunt.

DURING THE HUNGARIAN UPRISING

In crisis now I walk
The tidy troubled street
And every face I meet
Seems deeper than before
And when we stop and talk
Our sentences mean more.

Strangers as well as friends
Set subterfuge aside
And now refuse to hide.
What they hugged hard and near,
I mean their private ends,
On this day disappear.

Yet even so I see
Not general looks of pain,
Not eyes whose surface strain
Is like all other eyes:
The differences remain,
For all identities

Clutch at compassion which
Joins but can never make
Faces the same. We break
Towards each other. Here
In helpless grief we reach
And bear each other's fear.

ABSENCE

I visited the place where we last met.
Nothing was changed, the gardens were well-tended,
The fountains sprayed their usual steady jet;
There was no sign that anything had ended
And nothing to instruct me to forget.

The thoughtless birds that shook out of the trees,
Singing an ecstasy I could not share,
Played cunning in my thoughts. Surely in these
Pleasures there could not be a pain to bear
Or any discord shake the level breeze.

It was because the place was just the same
That made your absence seem a savage force,
For under all the gentleness there came
An earthquake tremor: fountain, birds and grass
Were shaken by my thinking of your name.

DISGUISES

Always we have believed
We can change overnight,
Put a different look on the face,
Old passions out of sight:
And find new days relieved
Of all that we regretted
But something always stays
And will not be outwitted.

Say we put on dark glasses,
Wear different clothes and walk
With a new unpractised stride—
Always somebody passes
Undeceived by disguises
Or the different way we talk.
And we who could have defied
Anything if it was strange
Have nowhere we can hide
From those who refuse to change.

THE PARTING

Though there was nothing final then,
No word or look or sign,
I felt some ending in the air
As when a sensed design
Draws back from the completing touch
And dies along a line.

For through the words that seemed to show
That we were learning each
Trick of the other's thought and sense,
A shyness seemed to reach
As if such talk continuing
Would make the hour too rich.

Maybe this strangeness only was
The safe place all men make
To hide themselves from happiness;
I only know I lack
The strangeness our last meeting had
And try to force it back.

RESEMBLANCES

Always I look for some reminding feature,
Compel a likeness where there is not one,
As in a gallery I trace the stature
Of that one's boldness or of this one's grace.
Yet likenesses so searched for will yield none;
One feature, yes, but never the whole face.

So every face falls back into its parts
And once-known glances leave the candid look
Of total strangeness. Where the likeness starts
We fix attention, set aside the rest,
As those who scan for notes a thick-packed book,
Recalling only what has pleased them best.

And doing this, so often I have missed
Some recognition never known before,
Some knowledge which I never could have guessed.
And how if all the others whom I pass
Should like myself be always searching for
The special features only one face has?

Always the dear enchanted moment stays.
We cannot unlearn all whom we have loved;
Who can tear off like calendars the days
Or wipe out features fixed within the mind?
Only there should be some way to be moved
Beyond the likeness to the look behind.

A DEATH

'His face shone' she said,
'Three days I had him in my house,
Three days before they took him from his bed,
And never have I felt so close.'

'Always alive he was
A little drawn away from me.
Looks are opaque when living and his face
Seemed hiding something, carefully.'

'But those three days before
They took his body out, I used to go
And talk to him. That shining from him bore
No secrets. Living, he never looked or answered so.'

Sceptic I listened, then
Noted what peace she seemed to have,
How tenderly she put flowers on his grave
But not as if he might return again
Or shine or seem quite close:
Rather to please us were the flowers she gave.

THE SHOT

The bullet shot me and I lay
So calm beneath the sun, the trees
Shook out their shadows in the breeze
Which carried half the sky away.

I did not know if I was dead,
A feeling close to sleep lay near
Yet through it I could see the clear
River and grass as if in bed

I lay and watched the morning come
Gentle behind the blowing stuff
Of curtains. But the pain was rough,
Not fitting to a sunlit room.

And I am dying, then, I thought.
I felt them lift me up and take
What seemed my body. Should I wake
And stop the darkness in my throat

And break the mist before my eyes?
I felt the bullet's leaps and swerves.
And none is loved as he deserves
And death is a disguise.

SONG FOR A DEPARTURE

Could you indeed come lightly
Leaving no mark at all
Even of footsteps, briefly
Visit not change the air
Of this or the other room,
Have quick words with us yet be
Calm and unhurried here?

So that we should not need—
When you departed lightly
Even as swift as coming
Letting no shadow fall—
Changes, surrenders, fear,
Speeches grave to the last,
But feel no loss at all?

Lightest things in the mind
Go deep at last and can never
Be planned or weighed or lightly
Considered or set apart.
Then come like a great procession,
Touch hours with drums and flutes:
Fill all the rooms of our houses
And haunt them when you depart.

CHOICES

Inside the room I see the table laid,
Four chairs, a patch of light the lamp has made

And people there so deep in tenderness
They could not speak a word of happiness.

Outside I stand and see my shadow drawn
Lengthening the clipped grass of the cared-for lawn.

Above, their roof holds half the sky behind.
A dog barks bringing distances to mind.

Comfort, I think, or safety then, or both?
I warm the cold air with my steady breath.

They have designed a way to live and I,
Clothed in confusion, set their choices by:

Though sometimes one looks up and sees me there,
Alerts his shadow, pushes back his chair

And, opening windows wide, looks out at me
And close past words we stare. It seems that he

Urges my darkness, dares it to be freed
Into that room. We need each other's need.

TELLING STORIES

FOR M.

Telling you stories I forget that you
Already know the end
And I forget that I am building up
A world in which no piece must be put back
In the wrong place or time
Else you will make me go back to the start.

My scope for improvising will not ever
Deceive you into taking
A change of plan. You are so grounded in
Your absolutes, even the worlds we build
Of thin thoughts, lean ideas
You will not let us alter but expect

The thing repeated whole. Is this then what
We call your innocence—
This fine decision not to have things changed?
Is this your way of stopping clocks, of damming
The thrusting stream of time?
Has a repeated story so much power?

Such is the trust you have not in large things
But in the placing of
A verb, an adjective, a happy end.
The stories that we tell, we tell against
Ourselves then at the last
Since all the worlds we make we stand outside

Leaning on time and swayed about by it
While you stand firm within the fragile plot.

A FEAR

Always to keep it in and never spare
Even a hint of pain, go guessing on,
Feigning a sacrifice, forging a tear
For someone else's grief, but still to bear
Inward the agony of self alone—

And all the masks I carry on my face,
The smile for you, the grave considered air
For you and for another some calm grace
When still within I carry an old fear
A child could never speak about, disgrace
That no confession could assuage or clear.

But once within a long and broken night
I woke and threw the shutters back for air
(The sudden moths were climbing to the light)
And from another window I saw stare
A face like mine still dream-bereft and white
And, like mine, shaken by a child's nightmare.

IN A FOREIGN CITY

You cannot speak for no-one knows
Your language. You must try to catch
By glances or by steadfast gaze
The attitude of those you watch.
No conversations can amaze:
Noises may find you but not speech.

Now you have circled silence, stare
With all the subtlety of sight.
Noise may trap ears but eye discerns
How someone on his elbow turns
And in the moon's long exile here
Touches another in the night.

THE ROMAN FORUM

Look at the Forum
Commanded now by Roman pines:
Walk down the ancient paths
Rubbed smooth by footprints in the past and now
Broken among the baths
And battered columns where the lizards go
In zig-zag movements like the lines
Of this decorum.

Not what the man
Who carved the column, reared the arch
Or shaped the buildings meant
Is what we marvel at. Perfection here
Is quite within our reach,
These ruins now are more than monument.
See how the houses disappear
Into a plan

Connived at by
Shadows of trees or light approved
By sun and not designed
By architects. Three columns eased away
From all support are moved
By how the shadows shake them from behind.
The pine trees droop their dark and sway
Swifter than eye

Can catch them all,
O and the heart is drawn to sense,
Eye and the mind are one.
The fragments here of former markets make
(Preserved by the intense
Glare of the Roman unremitting sun),

Such cities that the heart would break
And shadows fall

To see them pass.
Removed from Rome you, half-asleep,
Observe the shadows stray.
Above, the pines are playing with the light,
Dream now so dark and deep
That when you wake those columns, lucid, free,
Will burst like flowers into white
Springing from grass.

A CONVERSATION IN THE GARDENS OF THE VILLA CELIMONTANA, ROME

FOR A.

Deeper the shadows underneath the pines
Than their own trunks and roots. Under the hard
Blue of the sky (a Roman blue, they say)
I watched the afternoon weave its designs
Lucid as crystal on this first June day.

The fountains softly displayed themselves. The grass,
Unpressed by footprints yet, looked cool and young;
Over the paths we saw our shadows pass
And in the air the glittering moments strung
Together like a brilliance under glass.

Suddenly to this fullness our words went
Talking of visionaries, of those men
Who make a stillness deeper than an act,
Who probe beyond a place where passion's spent
And apprehend by purest intellect.

You talked of this and in between your words
I sensed (still shadowed by my own warm flesh)
That you had known such apprehension and
Back in this garden where the pine-trees stand
Held to that moment where all hungers hush.

Yes but the garden held a stillness too.
My mind could seize upon the pleasures there,
Yet in between the fountains and the grass,
The leaning pines, the overriding air,
I glimpsed a radiance where no shadows pass.

A ROMAN WINDOW

After the griefs of night,
Over the doors of day,
Here by this window-sill
I watch the climbing light
As early footsteps steal
Enormous shadows away.

Tenderly from this height
I feel compassion come—
People pestered by hours,
The morning swung to sight
As all the city stirs
And trembles in my room.

So from a stance of calm,
A stepping out of sleep,
My shadow once again
Disperses in the warm
Day with its lives more deep
Than any pleasure or pain.

FOUNTAIN

Let it disturb no more at first
Than the hint of a pool predicted far in a forest,
Or a sea so far away that you have to open
Your window to hear it.
Think of it then as elemental, as being
Necessity,
Not for a cup to be taken to it and not
For lips to linger or eye to receive itself
Back in reflection, simply
As water the patient moon persuades and stirs.

And then step closer,
Imagine rivers you might indeed embark on,
Waterfalls where you could
Silence an afternoon by staring but never
See the same tumult twice.
Yes come out of the narrow street and enter
The full piazza. Come where the noise compels.
Statues are bowing down to the breaking air.

Observe it there — the fountain, too fast for shadows,
Too wild for the lights which illuminate it to hold,
Even a moment, an ounce of water back;
Stare at such prodigality and consider
It is the elegance here, it is the taming,
The keeping fast in a thousand flowering sprays,
That builds this energy up but lets the watchers
See in that stress an image of utter calm,
A stillness there. It is how we must have felt
Once at the edge of some perpetual stream,
Fearful of touching, bringing no thirst at all,
Panicked by no perception of ourselves
But drawing the water down to the deepest wonder.

SANTA MARIA MAGGIORE, ROME

According to the legend, snow fell on the Esquiline Hill in August 358 A.D. as a sign that a great Basilica was to be built there

Say the snow drifted down
On the Esquiline Hill in August and the light
Easily changed to winter. Say the hill
Heaved for a moment over the town
And suddenly in the dear defeated night
The snow was still.

So I could well believe
Watching it now, the church completed there,
Altered and added to but still the same;
Senses and not the heart deceive—
Snow grown solid and grey in the Easter air.
I think there came

Once to the Pope and king
Who set the great basilica upright
A snowstorm in their hot and summer sleep
That when they woke they swore to bring
Such solid coolness to that sultry light
As snowdrifts deep.

SAN PAOLO FUORI LE MURA, ROME

It is the stone makes stillness here. I think
There could not be so much of silence if
The columns were not set there rank on rank,
For silence needs a shape in which to sink
And stillness needs these shadows for its life.

My darkness throws so little space before
My body where it stands, and yet my mind
Needs the large echoing churches and the roar
Of streets outside its own calm place to find
Where the soft doves of peace withdraw, withdraw.

The alabaster windows here permit
Only suggestions of the sun to slide
Into the church and make a glow in it;
The battering daylight leaps at large outside
Though what slips here through jewels seems most fit.

And here one might in his discovered calm
Feel the great building draw away from him,
His head bent closely down upon his arm,
With all the sun subsiding to a dim
Past-dreamt-of peace, a kind of coming home.

For me the senses still have their full sway
Even where prayer comes quicker than an act.
I cannot quite forget the blazing day,
The alabaster windows or the way
The light refuses to be called abstract.

LETTER FROM ASSISI

Here you will find peace, they said,
Here where silence is so wide you hear it,
Where every church you enter is a kind
Continuing of thought,
Here there is ease.
Now on this road, looking up to the hill
Where the town looks severe and seems to say
There is no softness here, no sensual joy,
Close by the flowers that fling me back to England—
The bleeding poppy and the dusty vetch
And all blue flowers reflecting back the sky—
It is not peace I feel but some nostalgia,
So that a hand which draws a shutter back,
An eye which warms as it observes a child,
Hurt me with homesickness. Peace pales and withers.

The doves demur, an English voice divides
The distances. It is the afternoon,
But here siesta has no place because
All of the day is strung with silences.
Bells wound the air and I remember one
Who long ago confided how such ringing
Brought salt into their mouth, tears to their eyes.
I think I understand a mood like that:
Doves, bells, the silent hills, O all the trappings
We dress our plans of peace in, fail me now.
I search some shadow wider than my own,
Some apprehension which requires no mood
Of local silence or a sense of prayer—
An open glance that looks from some high window
And illustrates a need I wish to share.

THE ANNUNCIATION

Nothing will ease the pain to come
Though now she sits in ecstasy
And lets it have its way with her.
The angel's shadow in the room
Is lightly lifted as if he
Had never terrified her there.

The furniture again returns
To its old simple state. She can
Take comfort from the things she knows
Though in her heart new loving burns
Something she never gave to man
Or god before, and this god grows

Most like a man. She wonders how
To pray at all, what thanks to give
And whom to give them to. 'Alone
To all men's eyes I now must go'
She thinks, 'And by myself must live
With a strange child that is my own.'

So from her ecstasy she moves
And turns to human things at last
(Announcing angels set aside).
It is a human child she loves
Though a god stirs beneath her breast
And great salvations grip her side.

THE VISITATION

She had not held her secret long enough
To covet it but wished it shared as though
Telling would tame the terrifying moment
When she, most calm in her own afternoon,
    Felt the intrepid angel, heard
His beating wings, his voice across her prayer.

This was the thing she needed to impart,
The uncalm moment, the strange interruption,
The angel bringing pain disguised as joy,
But mixed with this was something she could share
    And not abandon, simply how
A child sprang in her like the first of seeds.

And in the stillness of that other day
The afternoon exposed its emptiness,
Shadows adrift from light, the long road turning
In a dry sequence of the sun. And she
    No apprehensive figure seemed,
Only a moving silence through the land.

And all her journeying was a caressing
Within her mind of secrets to be spoken.
The simple fact of birth soon overshadowed
The shadow of the angel. When she came
    Close to her cousin's house she kept
Only the message of her happiness.

And those two women in their quick embrace
Gazed at each other with looks undisturbed
By men or miracles. It was the child
Who laid his shadow on their afternoon
    By stirring suddenly, by bringing
Back the broad echoes of those beating wings.

AGONY IN ANY GARDEN

And anybody's agony might be
This garden and this time. A different prayer,
A hand put out with no one else to touch
And faltering stammered words that cannot bear
The breadth of passion — anyone might reach
His pitch of hopelessness. We judge despair

By who cries out, by greatness underneath.
The dark night and the friends who would not wake
Are where we choose to place them. Now and here
Dumbness between thumped ribs may tear and break
And some small whimper shelter a great fear.

THE VIRGIN AT NOON

BY PAUL CLAUDEL

It is noon. I see that the church is open. I must go in.
Mother of Jesus Christ, I have not come to pray.

I have not come to offer anything or to ask for anything.
I come simply, Mother, to look at you.

To look at you, to weep with happiness, to know
That I am your son and that you are there.

Nothing happens for a moment: everything pauses.
Mid-day!
Be with us, Mary, in this place where you are.

There is nothing to say, I only want to look at your face
And let my heart sing in its own language.

There is nothing to speak about but only a need to sing
because the heart is too full,
Like the blackbird who delights himself with sudden
snatches of song.

Because you are beautiful, because you are spotless,
The girl in whom Grace is finally given back to us.

The creature in her first dignity and in her last flowering,
Such a one comes forth from God in the morning of her
original splendour.

Ineffably pure because you are the Mother of Jesus Christ
Who is the truth you carry in your arms and the only
hope and the only fruit.

Because you are the woman, the Eden of all ancient
forgotten tenderness,
The very contemplation of which suddenly pierces the
heart and makes all suppressed tears spring forth.

Because you have saved me, because you have saved France,
Because she also, like myself, was the thing which you cared for,
Because at the hour when everything failed, it was then
that you intervened,
Because you have saved France yet again,
Because it is noon, because we are in this day of days,
Because you are there always, simply because you are Mary,
simply because you exist,
Mother of Jesus Christ, accept my gratitude!

TERESA OF AVILA

Spain. The wild dust, the whipped corn, earth easy for footsteps, shallow to starving seeds. High sky at night like walls. Silences surrounding Avila.

She, teased by questions, aching for reassurance. Calm in confession before incredulous priests. Then back — to the pure illumination, the profound personal prayer, the four waters.

Water from the well first, drawn up painfully. Clinking of pails. Dry lips at the well-head. Parched grass bending. And the dry heart too — waiting for prayer.

Then the water-wheel, turning smoothly. Somebody helping unseen. A keen hand put out, gently sliding the wheel. Then water and the aghast spirit refreshed and quenched.

Not this only. Other waters also, clear from a spring or a pool. Pouring from a fountain like child's play — but the child is elsewhere. And she, kneeling, cooling her spirit at the water, comes nearer, nearer.

Then the entire cleansing, utterly from nowhere. No wind ruffled it, no shadows slid across it. Her mind met it, her will approved. And all beyonds, backwaters, dry words of old prayers were lost in it. The water was only itself.

And she knelt there, waited for shadows to cross the light which the water made, waited for familiar childhood illuminations (the lamp by the bed, the candle in church, sun beckoned by horizons) — but this light was none of these, was only how the water looked, how the will turned and was still. Even the image of light itself withdrew, and the dry dust on the winds of Spain outside her halted. Moments spread not into hours but stood still. No dove brought the tokens of peace. She was the peace that her prayer had promised. And the silences suffered no shadows.

SONG FOR A BIRTH OR A DEATH

1961

SONG FOR A BIRTH OR A DEATH

Last night I saw the savage world
And heard the blood beat up the stair;
The fox's bark, the owl's shrewd pounce,
The crying creatures — all were there,
And men in bed with love and fear.

The slit moon only emphasised
How blood must flow and teeth must grip.
What does the calm light understand,
The light which draws the tide and ship
And drags the owl upon its prey
And human creatures lip to lip?

Last night I watched how pleasure must
Leap from disaster with its will:
The fox's fear, the watch-dog's lust
Know that all matings mean a kill:
And human creatures kissed in trust
Feel the blood throb to death until

The seed is struck, the pleasure's done,
The birds are thronging in the air;
The moon gives way to widespread sun.
Yes but the pain still crouches where
The young fox and the child are trapped
And cries of love are cries of fear.

FAMILY AFFAIRS

No longer here the blaze that we'd engender
Out of pure wrath. We pick at quarrels now
As fussy women stitch at cotton, slow
Now to forget and too far to surrender.
The anger stops, apologies also.

And in this end of summer, weighted calm
(Climate of mind, I mean), we are apart
Further than ever when we wished most harm.
Indifference lays a cold hand on the heart;
We need the violence to keep us warm.

Have we then learnt at last how to untie
The bond of birth, umbilical long cord,
So that we live quite unconnected by
The blood we share? What monstrous kind of sword
Can sever veins and still we do not die?

A GAME OF CHESS

The quiet moves, the gently shaded room:
It is like childhood once again when I
Sat with a tray of toys and you would come
To take my temperature and make me lie
Under the clothes and sleep. Now peacefully

We sit above the intellectual game.
Pure mathematics seems to rule the board
Emotionless. And yet I feel the same
As when I sat and played without a word
Inventing kingdoms where great feelings stirred.

Is it that knight and king and small squat castle
Store up emotion, bring it under rule,
So that the problems now with which we wrestle
Seem simply of the mind? Do feelings cool
Beneath the order of an abstract school?

Never entirely, since the whole thing brings
Me back to childhood when I was distressed:
You seem the same who put away my things
At night, my toys and tools of childish lust.
My king is caught now in a world of trust.

MY GRANDMOTHER

She kept an antique shop — or it kept her.
Among Apostle spoons and Bristol glass,
The faded silks, the heavy furniture,
She watched her own reflection in the brass
Salvers and silver bowls, as if to prove
Polish was all, there was no need of love.

And I remember how I once refused
To go out with her, since I was afraid.
It was perhaps a wish not to be used
Like antique objects. Though she never said
That she was hurt, I still could feel the guilt
Of that refusal, guessing how she felt.

Later, too frail to keep a shop, she put
All her best things in one long narrow room.
The place smelt old, of things too long kept shut,
The smell of absences where shadows come
That can't be polished. There was nothing then
To give her own reflection back again.

And when she died I felt no grief at all,
Only the guilt of what I once refused.
I walked into her room among the tall
Sideboards and cupboards — things she never used
But needed: and no finger-marks were there,
Only the new dust falling through the air.

IN PRAISE OF CREATION

That one bird, one star,
The one flash of the tiger's eye
Purely assert what they are,
Without ceremony testify.

Testify to order, to rule—
How the birds mate at one time only,
How the sky is, for a certain time, full
Of birds, the moon sometimes cut thinly.

And the tiger trapped in the cage of his skin,
Watchful over creation, rests
For the blood to pound, the drums to begin,
Till the tigress' shadow casts

A darkness over him, a passion, a scent,
The world goes turning, turning, the season
Sieves earth to its one sure element
And the blood beats beyond reason.

Then quiet, and birds folding their wings,
The new moon waiting for years to be stared at here,
The season sinks to satisfied things—
Man with his mind ajar.

WORLD I HAVE NOT MADE

I have sometimes thought how it would have been
if I had had to create the whole thing myself—
my life certainly but also something else;
I mean a world which I could inhabit freely,
ideas, objects, everything prepared;
not ideas simply as Plato knew them,
shadows of shadows, but more like furniture,
something to move around and live in,
something *I* had made. But still there would be
all that I hadn't made—animals, stars,
tides tugging against me, moon uncaring,
and the trying to love without reciprocity.
All this is here still. It is hard, hard,
even with free faith outlooking boundaries,
to come to terms with obvious suffering.
I live in a world I have not created
inward or outward. There is a sweetness
in willing surrender: I trail my ideas
behind great truths. My ideas are like shadows
and sometimes I consider how it would have been
to create a credo, objects, ideas
and then to live with them. I can understand
when tides most tug and the moon is remote
and the trapped wild beast is one with its shadow,
how even great faith leaves room for abysses
and the taut mind turns to its own requirings.

HARVEST AND CONSECRATION

After the heaped piles and the cornsheaves waiting
To be collected, gathered into barns,
After all fruits have burst their skins, the sating
  Season cools and turns,
And then I think of something that you said
Of when you held the chalice and the bread.

I spoke of Mass and thought of it as close
To how a season feels which stirs and brings
Fire to the hearth, food to the hungry house
  And strange, uncovered things—
God in a garden then in sheaves of corn
And the white bread a way to be reborn.

I thought of priest as midwife and as mother
Feeling the pain, feeling the pleasure too,
  All opposites together,
Until you said no one could feel such passion
And still preserve the power of consecration.

And it is true. How cool the gold sheaves lie,
Rich without need to ask for any more
Richness. The seed, the simple thing must die
  If only to restore
Our faith in fruitful, hidden things. I see
The wine and bread protect our ecstasy.

A WORLD OF LIGHT

Yes when the dark withdrew I suffered light
And saw the candles heave beneath their wax,
I watched the shadow of my old self dwindle
As softly on my recollection stole
A mood the senses could not touch or damage,
A sense of peace beyond the breathing word.

Day dawdled at my elbow. It was night
Within. I saw my hands, their soft dark backs
Keeping me from the noise outside. The candle
Seemed snuffed into a deep and silent pool:
It drew no shadow round my constant image
For in a dazzling dark my spirit stirred.

But still I questioned it. My inward sight
Still knew the senses and the senses' tracks,
I felt my flesh and clothes, a rubbing sandal,
And distant voices wishing to console.
My mind was keen to understand and rummage
To find assurance in the sounds I heard.

Then senses ceased and thoughts were driven quite
Away (no act of mine). I could relax
And feel a fire no earnest prayer can kindle;
Old parts of peace dissolved into a whole
And like a bright thing proud in its new plumage
My mind was keen as an attentive bird.

Yes, fire, light, air, birds, wax, the sun's own height
I draw from now, but every image breaks.
Only a child's simplicity can handle
Such moments when the hottest fire feels cool,
And every breath is like a sudden homage
To peace that penetrates and is not feared.

NOTES FOR A BOOK OF HOURS

I

Kneeling to pray and resting on the words
I feel a stillness that I have not made.
Shadows take root, the falling light is laid
Smoothly on stone and skin. I lean towards
Some meaning that's delayed.

It is as if the mind had nervous fingers,
Could touch and apprehend yet not possess.
The light is buried where the darkness lingers
And something grateful in me wants to bless
Simply from happiness.

The world dreams through me in this sudden spring.
My senses itch although the stillness stays.
God is too large a word for me to sing,
Some touch upon my spirit strums and plays:
What images will bring

This moment down to words that I can use
When not so rapt? The hours, the hours increase.
All is a movement, shadows now confuse,
Darkening the soft wings of the doves of peace,
And can I tame or choose?

NOTES FOR A BOOK OF HOURS

II

I have to start the whole thing from the source,
Go back behind the noisy tower of tongues,
Press on my words new meanings, make my songs
Like breath from uncontaminated lungs
Or water from a new-found water-course.

Not to convince you, that it is not my aim,
Simply to speak and to be gladly heard.
I have the oils, the waters, but the name
Eludes me still. Within a single word
I want the christening, the flowering flame.

Men had it once who carved far out of sight
Demons and angels, all anonymous;
Skill was another name for pure delight.
My angels must convince, be obvious.
I must create the substance and the light.

The cosmic vision fades. Within my mind
The images are laid, books on a shelf
Dusty and old. I only need to find
Some way to show the struggle in myself —
The demons watchful but the angels blind.

NOTES FOR A BOOK OF HOURS

III

In the cool cloisters and the choirs I hear
The open-handed words, the pleading psalms.
The chant is sober and it soothes and calms
Though what the words depict is full of fear;
I gather all the shadows in my arms.

I cannot sing but only hear and trace
The meaning underneath the echoes, wait
For the resumption of a scattered state.
Such concentration screwed into my face —
Can it reflect an inner mood of grace?

What do they think who kneel within those stalls,
Young, old, white, black? The world outside still gropes
Not for a paradise but for its hopes
Come true in time. The chanting sinks and falls —
The great bell silent, none to pull the ropes.

NOTES FOR A BOOK OF HOURS

IV

The sound is ordered, cool.
I heard somebody say
Once that the liturgy is diffused
Theology. I think they meant the way
The music and the words are used,
Austere yet beautiful.

A world of dogma can
Within these hours be pressed.
Both day and night are counted by
The times of exhortation and of rest.
The psalms can both rejoice and sigh,
Serve every need of man.

I need to make my own
Great books of hours, record
Matins and lauds, prime, terce and vespers,
With no authority but my own word.
The psalms are loud with truth; in whispers
I mark my hours alone.

A CONFESSION

It seemed the most unlikely place to bring
One's childhood back. Outside, the grown world clung
To light, or did the light engender it?
Within the church, all that was old revived—
Gold on the roof, and in the shining apse
Mosaics stood within a lively stillness.
All was perpetual and precious here.

And here a foreigner, though recognised
By gentleness that leaps ahead of language,
I could discourse of every shameful topic,
Reveal the secret passions of a childhood,
Speak, fumblingly, the fears of adolescence.
And still the gold mosaics went on shining
And still, outside, the city played with light.

Exiles, perhaps, are people without shadows,
Movers beyond the sequences of time.
Simply to speak here is to be accepted.
Or does the light play tricks with one's own past,
Show it unshameful? Does one here mark time
Not with the stamping foot's impatient beat
But with surrender, attribute of love?

A REQUIEM

It is the ritual not the fact
That brings a held emotion to
Its breaking-point. This man I knew
Only a little, by his death
Shows me a love I thought I lacked
And all the stirrings underneath.

It is the calm, the solemn thing,
Not the distracted mourners cry
Or the cold place where dead things lie,
That teaches me I cannot claim
To stand aside. These tears which sting—
Are they from sorrow or from shame?

AT A MASS

Waiting restlessly the coming event,
Hearing the three bells ringing the loud warning,
I look for the lifted moment, the lifted cup,
Feeling upon my skin the Roman morning.
I watch with a critical eye the bread raised up
And confuse aesthetics now with a sacrament.

It is the veils drawn over, the decent hiding
That recall the decorum the test of art demands.
Around me the people pray, forgetful of
Even their painful eyes, their well-worn hands.
I struggle now with my own ideas of love
And wonder if art and religion mean dividing.

Each has his way and mine perhaps is to
Suffer the critical sense that cannot rest.
If the air is cool, the colours right, the spoken
Words dramatic enough, then I am pleased.
But why must I ask a sense of style in the broken
Bread and bring God down to my limited view?

Pride enfolds me, pride in the gift of tongues;
Envy too, since I long to be like these
Who approach with empty hands, an open heart—
The simple men lost in simplicities.
I have to endure the ecstatic pain of art
And shape from the silence all my encroaching songs.

JOHN OF THE CROSS

Emptiness, space. Darkness you could put walls round, set stars in, light from far off but never unthinkingly enter. To approach was to become the darkness, not even assisted by shadows.

And the senses, too, disarmed, discouraged, withdrawn by choice from pleasure. Fingers not touching, crushing cool leaves. Lips closed against mouth or assuagement. Ears unentered by voices. Hands held out but empty. Even the darkness could not be possessed.

All indescribable then, but still the urge to depict, descry, point out, picture, prepare. The deep darkness had to be spoken of, touched beyond reach of stars, entered without indications.

Flame, then, firm — not the inward flame of passion, urgent, wanting appeasement, close to the senses and sighing through them: but a pure light pouring through windows, flooding the glass but leaving the glass unaltered.

More than this too. Not light limited by tapers, drawn to its strength by the darkness around it, not puffed out by wind or increased by careful breath.

It is held in being by patience, by watching, suffering beyond signs or words. Not your light either. You are receiver, requirer. And when the flame falters nothing of yours can revive it: you are resigned to the darkness. And you open your eyes to the world.

THE RESURRECTION

I was the one who waited in the garden
Doubting the morning and the early light.
I watched the mist lift off its own soft burden,
Permitting not believing my own sight.

If there were sudden noises I dismissed
Them as a trick of sound, a sleight of hand.
Not by a natural joy could I be blessed
Or trust a thing I could not understand.

Maybe I was a shadow thrown by one
Who, weeping, came to lift away the stone,
Or was I but the path on which the sun,
Too heavy for itself, was loosed and thrown?

I heard the voices and the recognition
And love like kisses heard behind thin walls.
Were they my tears which fell, a real contrition?
Or simply April with its waterfalls?

It was by negatives I learnt my place.
The garden went on growing and I sensed
A sudden breeze that blew across my face.
Despair returned but now it danced, it danced.

MANTEGNA'S *AGONY IN THE GARDEN*

The agony is formal; three
Bodies are stretched in pure repose,
One's halo leans against a tree,
Over a book his fingers close:
One's arms are folded carefully.

The third man lies with sandalled feet
Thrust in the path. They almost touch
Three playful rabbits. Down the street,
Judas and his procession march
Making the distance seem discreet.

Even the praying figure has
A cared-for attitude. This art
Puts down the city and the mass
Of mountains like a counterpart
Of pain disguised as gentleness.

And yet such careful placing here
Of mountain, men and agony,
Being so solid makes more clear
The pain. Pain is particular.
The foreground shows a barren tree:
Is it a vulture crouching there,
No symbol but a prophecy?

THE RETREAT

Here in this room, the very top of the tower,
I live a little. On these checkered walls
Some past is written and some ancient power
Is whispered in those finger-marks and scrawls—
Childhood or family history or war?
Or were the things inventions, always false?

One window, steep enough to hold the sky,
Holds the sea too; today the water's calm,
The cumbered breakers have smoothed out and lie
As if no ripple cut across their firm
And balanced movement. Meanwhile, slowly I
Sit meditating, head upon my arm.

Silence is spread for me and no one knows
That I am here; no one can point and say
'Escaper both from failure and applause.'
The tongues of fire have not come down today
Nor the descending doves of peace. I close
My door and make my peace in my own way.

And shall be better when I climb the stairs
Downward to darkness and the still-calm sea.
Voices will snatch me and the old despairs
Return. One moment, recollectedly
I understand old silences and prayers
Yet know that something else is meant for me.

VISIT TO AN ARTIST

FOR DAVID JONES

Window upon the wall, a balcony
With a light chair, the air and water so
Mingled you could not say which was the sun
And which the adamant yet tranquil spray.
But nothing was confused and nothing slow:
Each way you looked always the sea, the sea.

And every shyness that we brought with us
Was drawn into the pictures on the walls.
It was so good to sit quite still and lose
Necessity of discourse, words to choose
And wonder which were honest and which false.

Then I remembered words that you had said
Of art as gesture and as sacrament,
A mountain under the calm form of paint
Much like the Presence under wine and bread—
Art with its largesse and its own restraint.

THE CLOWN

I

Balloon on finger he watches us, the clown;
White cheeks conceal what eyes are witness of
And nimble body hides in pantaloon.
If you love this it is yourself you love,
Your own absurdity, your pride brought down.

But is this what he means, or does he mean
A dancing childish world where play is fact?
The rubber ball returns unburst and clean —
Your world so shapely, blown up but intact?
Are you the dancer in a pasteboard scene.

I am afraid of things which can be hurt.
The clown as much as cringing animals
Invites my wounding. Yet my pain will start
Because I wound. The clown prevails in art;
Gently as his balloon, my pity falls.

THE CLOWN

II

Aloof, reserved, yet strangely vulnerable,
Making of art a nonchalance, mere skill

As though a skill were something not to care
Too much about. You throw balls in the air,

You make yourself ridiculous, your face
Fitting nowhere but in a taut white space.

Yet sometimes carelessly you have been drawn
By painters in their note-book moments when

A special care appears but fits nowhere —
A harlequin who leans upon a chair,

A youth who idly strums an old guitar,
Each lazy gesture meaning 'I don't care.'

THE CLOWN

III

Others are noble and admired—
The ones who walk the tightrope without nets,
The one who goes inside the lion's cage,
And all the grave, audacious acrobats.
Away from fear and rage
He simply is the interval for tired

People who cannot bear
Too much excitement. They can see in him
Their own lost innocence or else their fear
(For him no metal bars or broken limb).
Have they forgotten that it takes as much
Boldness to tumble, entertain and jest
When loneliness walks tightropes in your breast
And every joke is like a wild beast's touch?

THE CLOWN

IV

If I painted you
It would not be as juggler or as one who
Played the fool and entertained the crowds.
I would have you entirely alone,
Thoughtful and leaning
Against a dark window that needed cleaning.

I would want to show you
Not as victim or scapegoat,
Not like one who is hurried away, loaded
With other people's fears, goaded
Into the distance, but rather
As one who uses distance as a tether,
Tied but detached,
Sympathetic yet remote.

Strangely you remind
Of Christ on the cross.
Is it the seeming surrender or the white face,
The acceptance of loss?
Or simply that you seem like one not fallen from grace,
Innocent through knowledge,
Assenting yet resigned?

THE CLOWN

V

The eager one unconscious of himself,
Drawing the bow across the strings, absorbed
In music or the version that he makes,

The smiling one who never seems afraid,
Something to offer always yet not hoarding
His own or others' thoughts of what he is—

Simply the one who does not analyse
But still can gauge the feelings that surround him,
Loosen the taut voice, spread the narrow smile.

My childhood stands abruptly at my elbow
Forbidding demonstration, looking in,
Seeing the wishes and the dancers there.

THE CLOWN

VI

Something he has to say
Concerning pain. You have to watch the dance
With utmost concentration, in the way
A child will watch until the view enchants
And he is lost in it. The clown is gay
And terrible at once.

His face will never show
You any hint of what you ought to feel:
White greasepaint spreads across his cheeks like snow.
His jokes seem feeble and his tricks are slow,
He seems a game, unreal.

And yet his helplessness,
His lack of tragic gesture, tragic mood,
Remind me of the abject beast we press
Our own despairs on, Christ nailed to the wood.
There are more ways to make a wilderness
Than we have understood.

LAZARUS

It was the amazing white, it was the way he simply
Refused to answer our questions, it was the cold pale glance
Of death upon him, the smell of death that truly
Declared his rising to us. It was no chance
Happening, as a man may fill a silence
Between two heart-beats, seem to be dead and then
Astonish us with the closeness of his presence;
This man was dead, I say it again and again.
All of our sweating bodies moved towards him
And our minds moved too, hungry for finished faith.
He would not enter our world at once with words
That we might be tempted to twist or argue with:
Cold like a white root pressed in the bowels of earth
He looked, but also vulnerable—like birth.

THE DIAMOND CUTTER

Not what the light will do but how he shapes it
And what particular colours it will bear,

And something of the climber's concentration
Seeing the white peak, setting the right foot there.

Not how the sun was plausible at morning
Nor how it was distributed at noon,

And not how much the single stone could show
But rather how much brilliance it would shun;

Simply a paring down, a cleaving to
One object, as the star-gazer who sees

One single comet polished by its fall
Rather than countless, untouched galaxies.

STARGAZERS AND OTHERS

One, staring out stars,
Lost himself in looking and almost
Forgot glass, eye, air, space;
Simply, he thought, the world is improved
By my staring, how the still glass leaps
When the sky thuds in like tides.

Another, making love, once
Stared so far over his pleasure
That woman, world, the spiral
Of taut bodies, the clinging hands, broke apart
And he saw, as the stargazer sees,
Landscapes made to be looked at,
Fruit to fall, not be plucked.

In you also something
Of such vision occurs.
How else would I have learnt
The tapered stars, the pause
On the nervous spiral? Names I need
Stronger than love, desire,
Passion, pleasure. Oh discover
Some star and christen it, but let me be
The space that your eye moves over.

TO A FRIEND WITH A RELIGIOUS VOCATION

FOR C.

Thinking of your vocation, I am filled
With thoughts of my own lack of one. I see
Within myself no wish to breed or build
Or take the three vows ringed by poverty.
        And yet I have a sense,
Vague and inchoate, with no symmetry,
Of purpose. Is it merely a pretence,

A kind of scaffolding which I erect
Half out of fear, half out of laziness?
The fitful poems come but can't protect
The empty areas of loneliness?
        You know what you must do,
So that mere breathing is a way to bless.
Dark nights, perhaps, but no grey days for you.

Your vows enfold you. I must make my own;
Now this, now that, each one empirical.
My poems move from feelings not yet known,
And when the poem is written I can feel
        A flash, a moment's peace.
The curtain will be drawn across your grille.
My silences are always enemies.

Yet with the same convictions that you have
(It is but your vocation that I lack),
I must, like you, believe in perfect love.
It is the dark, the dark that draws me back
        Into a chaos where
Vocations, visions fail, the will grows slack
And I am stunned by silence everywhere.

GREEK STATUES

These I have never touched but only looked at.
If you could say that stillness meant surrender
These are surrendered.
Yet their large audacious gestures signify surely
Remonstrance, reprisal? What have they left to lose
But the crumbling away by rain or time? Defiance
For them is a dignity, a declaration.

Odd how one wants to touch not simply stare,
To run one's fingers over the flanks and arms,
Not to possess, rather to be possessed.
Bronze is bright to the eye but under the hands
Is cool and calming. Gods into silent metal:

To stone also, not to the palpable flesh.
Incarnations are elsewhere and more human,
Something concerning us; but these are other.
It is as if something infinite, remote
Permitted intrusion. It is as if these blind eyes
Exposed a landscape precious with grapes and olives:
And our probing hands move not to grasp but praise.

THE PRIDE OF LIFE: A ROMAN SETTING

Old men discourse upon wise topics here:
Children and women pass the shadows by,
Only the young are desperate. Their clear
And unambiguous gazes strike
Against each brushing hand or eye,
Their faces like

O something far away, maybe a cave
Where looks and actions always moved to hunt,
Where every gesture knew how to behave
And there was never space between
The easy having and the want.
I think the keen

Primitive stares that pierce this decorous street
Look to some far back mood and time to claim
A life beyond the urbane and effete
Where youth from coolest childhood came,
And look to look was like the hunter's throw —
Perpetually new and long ago.

MEN FISHING IN THE ARNO

I do not know what they are catching,
I only know that they stand there, leaning
A little like lovers, eager but not demanding,
Waiting and hoping for a catch, money,
A meal tomorrow but today, still there, steady.

And the river also moves as calmly
From the waterfall slipping to a place
A mind could match its thought with.
And above, the cypresses with cool gestures
Command the city, give it formality.

It is like this every day but more especially
On Sundays; every few yards you see a fisherman,
Each independent, none
Working with others and yet accepting
Others. From this one might, I think,

Build a whole way of living — men in their mazes
Of secret desires yet keeping a sense
Of order outwardly, hoping
Not too flamboyantly, satisfied with little
Yet not surprised should the river suddenly
Yield a hundredfold, every hunger appeased.

TWO DEATHS

It was only a film,
Perhaps I shall say later
Forgetting the story, left only
With bright images — the blazing dawn
Over the European ravaged plain,
And a white unsaddled horse, the only calm
Living creature. Will only such pictures remain?

Or shall I see
The shot boy running, running
Clutching the white sheet on the washing-line,
Looking at his own blood like a child
Who never saw blood before and feels defiled,
A boy dying without dignity
Yet brave still, trying to stop himself from falling
And screaming — his white girl waiting just out of calling?

I am ashamed
Not to have seen anyone dead,
Anyone I know I mean;
Odd that yesterday also
I saw a broken cat stretched on a path,
Not quite finished. Its gentle head
Showed one eye staring, mutely beseeching
Death, it seemed. All day
I have thought of death, of violence and death,
Of the blazing Polish light, of the cat's eye:
I am ashamed I have never seen anyone die.

ABOUT THESE THINGS

About these things I always shall be dumb.
Some wear their silences as more than dress,
As more than skin-deep. I bear mine like some

Scar that is hidden out of shamefulness.
I speak from depths I do not understand
Yet cannot find the words for this distress.

So much of power is put into my hand
When words come easily. I sense the way
People are charmed and pause; I seem to mend

Some hurt. Some healing seems to make them stay.
And yet within the power that I use
My wordless fears remain. Perhaps I say

In lucid verse the terrors that confuse
In conversation. Maybe I am dumb
Because if fears were spoken I would lose

The lovely languages I do not choose
More than the darknesses from which they come.

NO REPLY

Between acceptance and the sense of loss
I pause, reluctant to admit the blame.
Leaves lie along the streets as if to gloss
A grief they never knew, could never name.
I watch them, knowing I am still the same.

Love has its battles and its counterparts
But friendship has to make rules of its own
Both for betrayals and for broken hearts,
Also for feelings that were never shown;
Emotion's not explained by thought alone.

Love could be stressed in touches and in looks.
We only have the easy words we say
When close together. Words seem out of books
When there is any absence or delay;
Distances not ourselves, perhaps, betray.

My letters go, hectic with crossings-out,
Having no substitute for pause in speech.
I wait for answers, building out of doubt
More feeling than mere friendships ever reach,
Learning a lesson I would fear to teach.

THE UNFULFILLED

It was love only that we knew
At first. We did not dispossess
Each other of the total view
That is quite blurred when passions pass.
I felt myself, acknowledged you.

When did desire enter and
Confuse the sweetness, heat the blood?
On meeting we could understand,
Wordless, each other's every mood.
Where does love start and friendship end?

Impediments have set apart
The impulse from fruition. We,
Who have no compass but the heart,
Must learn an immaturity,
Though all the later passions hurt.

By acts of will we now must find
Each other as we were at first,
Unthwarted then and unconfined.
Yes, but I have an aching thirst
That can't be quenched by a cool mind.

We must stand side by side and live
As if the past were still to come.
It is our needs we need to give
And fashion from their anguish some
Love that has no wish to deceive
But rests contented, being dumb.

NO CHILD

We touch and when our hands
Meet, a world rises up,
A hemisphere extends,
Rivers we cannot stop.
Yet something is withheld —
No marriage and no child.

Our fields that seem so thick
With corn, that make an edge
Of gold, play us a trick;
It is a barren hedge,
A stony, sterile field:
No marriage and no child.

Yet barrenness also
Is tender. Others give
To children what we show
Each other. We can live
Sufficiently fulfilled,
No marriage and no child.

And what a child might take
In flesh and blood and mind
To the edge of heartbreak,
We hand over and find
That each of us can build
Out of this love, a child.

THE INSTRUMENTS

Only in our imaginations
The act is done, for you have spoken
Vows that can never now be broken.
I keep them too — with reservations;
Yet acts not done can still be taken
Away, like all completed passions.

But what can not be taken is
Satiety. Cool space lies near
Our bodies — a parenthesis
Between a pleasure and a fear.
Our loving is composed of this
Touching of strings to make sounds clear.

A touching, then a glancing off.
It is your vows that stretch between
Us like an instrument of love
Where only echoes intervene.
Yet these exchanges are enough
Since strings touched only are most keen.

REMEMBERING FIREWORKS

Always as if for the first time we watch
The fireworks as if no one had ever
Done this before, made shapes, signs,
Cut diamonds on air, sent up stars
Nameless, imperious. And in the falling
Of fire, the spent rocket, there is a kind
Of nostalgia as normally only attaches
To things long known and lost. Such an absence,
Such emptiness of sky the fireworks leave
After their festival. We, fumbling
For words of love, remember the rockets,
The spinning wheels, the sudden diamonds,
And say with delight 'Yes, like that, like that.'
Oh and the air is full of falling
Stars surrendered. We search for a sign.

RECOVERIES

1964

SEQUENCE IN HOSPITAL

I PAIN

At my wits' end
And all resources gone, I lie here,
All of my body tense to the touch of fear,
And my mind,

Muffled now as if the nerves
Refused any longer to let thoughts form,
Is no longer a safe retreat, a tidy home,
No longer serves

My body's demands or shields
With fine words, as it once would daily,
My storehouse of dread. Now, slowly,
My heart, hand, whole body yield

To fear. Bed, ward, window begin
To lose their solidity. Faces no longer
Look kind of needed; yet I still fight the stronger
Terror — oblivion — the needle thrusts in.

II THE WARD

One with the photographs of grandchildren,
Another with discussion of disease,

Another with the memory of her garden,
Another with her marriage—all of these

Keep death at bay by building round their illness
A past they never honoured at the time.

The sun streams through the window, the earth heaves
Gently for this new season. Blossoms climb

Out in the healthy world where no one thinks
Of pain. Nor would these patients wish them to;

The great preservers here are little things—
The dream last night, a photograph, a view.

III AFTER AN OPERATION

What to say first? I learnt I was afraid,
Not frightened in the way that I had been
When wide awake and well. I simply mean
Fear became absolute and I became
Subject to it; it beckoned, I obeyed.

Fear which before had been particular,
Attached to this or that scene, word, event,
Here became general. Past, future meant
Nothing. Only the present moment bore
This huge, vague fear, this wish for nothing more.

Yet life still stirred and nerves themselves became
Like shoots which hurt while growing, sensitive
To find not death but further ways to live.
And now I'm convalescent, fear can claim
No general power. Yet I am not the same.

IV PATIENTS IN A PUBLIC WARD

Like children now, bed close to bed,
With flowers set up where toys would be
In real childhoods, secretly
We cherish each our own disease,
And when we talk we talk to please
Ourselves that still we are not dead.

All is kept safe — the healthy world
Held at a distance, on a rope,
Where human things like hate and hope
Persist. The world we know is full
Of things we need, unbeautiful
And yet desired — a glass to hold

And sip, a cube of ice, a pill
To help us sleep. Yet in this warm
And sealed-off nest, the least alarm
Speaks clear of death. Our fears grow wide;
There are no places left to hide
And no more peace in lying still.

V THE VISITORS

They visit me and I attempt to keep
A social smile upon my face. Even here
Some ceremony is required, no deep
Relationship, simply a way to clear
    Emotion to one side; the fear
I felt last night is buried in drugged sleep.

They come and all their kindness makes me want
To cry (they say the sick weep easily).
When they have gone I shall be limp and faint,
My heart will thump and stumble crazily;
    Yet through my illness I can see
One wish stand clear no pain, no fear can taint.

Your absence has been stronger than all pain
And I am glad to find that when most weak
Always my mind returned to you again.
Through all the noisy nights when, harsh awake,
    I longed for day and light to break—
In that sick desert, you were life, were rain.

VI HOSPITAL

Observe the hours which seem to stand
Between these beds and pause until
A shriek breaks through the time to show
That humankind is suffering still.

Observe the tall and shrivelled flowers,
So brave a moment to the glance.
The fevered eyes stare through the hours
And petals fall with soft foot-prints.

A world where silence has no hold
Exceptive a tentative small grip.
Limp hands upon the blankets fold,
Minds from their bodies slowly slip.

Though death is never talked of here,
It is more palpable and felt—
Touching the cheek or in a tear—
By being present by default.

The muffled cries, the curtains drawn,
The flowers pale before they fall—
The world itself is here brought down
To what is suffering and small.

The huge philosophies depart,
Large words slink off, like faith, like love.
The thumping of the human heart
Is reassurance here enough.

Only one dreamer going back
To how he felt when he was well,
Weeps under pillows at his lack
But cannot tell, but cannot tell.

VII FOR A WOMAN WITH A FATAL ILLNESS

The verdict has been given and you lie quietly
Beyond hope, hate, revenge, even self-pity.

You accept gratefully the gifts — flowers, fruit —
Clumsily offered now that your visitors too

Know you must certainly die in a matter of months,
They are dumb now, reduced only to gestures,

Helpless before your news, perhaps hating
You because you are the cause of their unease.

I, too, watching from my temporary corner,
Feel impotent and wish for something violent —

Whether as sympathy only, I am not sure —
But something at least to break the terrible tension.

Death has no right to come so quietly.

VIII PATIENTS

Violence does not terrify.
Storms here would be a relief,
Lightning be a companion to grief.
It is the helplessness, the way they lie

Beyond hope, fear, love,
That makes me afraid. I would like to shout,
Crash my voice into the silence, flout
The passive suffering here. They move

Only in pain, their bodies no longer seem
Dependent on blood, muscle, bone.
It is as if air alone
Kept them alive, or else a mere whim

On the part of instrument, surgeon, nurse.
I too am one of them, but well enough
To long for some simple sign of life,
Or to imagine myself getting worse.

NERVES

The wind is playing round the curtains,
The bowl of flowers throws shadows on the sill.
There is nothing to do now, nothing at all
But to lie still.

The mind has never been like this room, clear,
Containing only what I really need.
It has been full of antique objects, rubbish,
And dust indeed.

The objects seemed to swell, their shadows spread
More darkness than I knew how I could handle.
There was no sudden shock, simply a slow
Feeling that strength would dwindle,

That I would one day find myself like this —
Lying in bed, watching the curtains blow,
Seeing the flowers fall, petal by petal,
Longing for something to grow.

WORKS OF ART

So often it appears like an escape,
That cool, wide world where even shadows are
Ordered and relegated to a shape
Not too intrusive and yet not too spare.
How easy it has seemed to wander deep
Into this world and find a shelter there.

Yet always it surprises. Nervous hands
Which make the first rough sketch in any art,
Leave their own tension, and the statue stands,
The poem lies with trouble at its heart.
And every fashioned object makes demands
Though we feel uncommitted at the start.

Yeats said that gaiety explained it all,
That Hamlet, Lear were gay, and so are we.
He did not look back to a happy Fall
Where man stood lost, ashamed beneath a tree.
There was no art within that garden wall
Until we chose our dangerous liberty.

And now all making has the bitter-sweet
Taste of frustration yet of something done.
We want more order than we ever meet
And art keeps driving us most hopefully on.
Yet coolness is derived from all that heat,
And shadows draw attention to the sun.

MAN IN A PARK

One lost in thought of what his life might mean
Sat in a park and watched the children play,
Did nothing, spoke to no one, but all day
Composed his life around the happy scene.

And when the sun went down and keepers came
To lock the gates, and all the voices were
Swept to a distance where no sounds could stir,
This man continued playing his odd game.

Thus, without protest, he went to the gate,
Heard the key turn and shut his eyes until
He felt that he had made the whole place still,
Being content simply to watch and wait.

So one can live, like patterns under glass,
And, like those patterns, not committing harm.
This man continued faithful to his calm,
Watching the children playing on the grass.

But what if someone else should also sit
Beside him on the bench and play the same
Watching and counting, self-preserving game,
Building a world with him no part of it?

If he is truthful to his vision he
Will let the dark intruder push him from
His place, and in the softly gathering gloom
Add one more note to his philosophy.

STILL LIFE AND OBSERVER

The jar
Holds the shadows.
The shining apple
Exults in its own being,
Exacts
Not appetite but observation.
The light folds, joins,
Separates.
Here energy is in abeyance,
Silence is tamed and tethered.
The one observer
(Himself almost a still life)
Watches eagerly but quietly,
Content to let the light be the only movement,
The shadows the only interruption.
Not the objects here but their setting
Is what is important.
So with the observer,
Whose slightest movement will shift the shadows,
Whose gaze balances the objects.

FATHER TO SON

I do not understand this child
Though we have lived together now
In the same house for years. I know
Nothing of him, so try to build
Up a relationship from how
He was when small. Yet have I killed

The seed I spent or sown it where
The land is his and none of mine?
We speak like strangers, there's no sign
Of understanding in the air.
This child is built to my design
Yet what he loves I cannot share.

Silence surrounds us. I would have
Him prodigal, returning to
His father's house, the home he knew,
Rather than see him make and move
His world. I would forgive him too,
Shaping from sorrow a new love.

Father and son, we both must live
On the same globe and the same land.
He speaks: I cannot understand
Myself, why anger grows from grief.
We each put out an empty hand,
Longing for something to forgive.

FOR A VISIONARY POET

You will expect the light to come to hand
As birds to other men; you will demand
(So gently that it seems a mere suggestion)
An image to impose itself: for instance,
This middle-light that in September glows
Half-way between the earth and trees, a point
Where things fall down or rise, say fruit, or smoke.

You gather and possess, since your detachment
Looks out for words, asks you to annotate.
Light least infringes on the fragile view
And keeps the meaning. Fractured glass also
Serves for a symbol. You will find a use
For any light that falls, especially
The calming glow that does not burn to ash.

It is an aristocracy of style
You seek, the perfect object, artifice
That shows no touch of human hands but bears
Only the weight of history, tradition.
You are the history behind your vision,
The shadow that you will not let intrude
Except that it makes all light impossible.

EXODUS

I

Down from the cliffs we came. Hand in hand. Children with all afternoons before us. The tide was out and the rocks were shining. We had nets for shrimping and bare feet.

The war was a sea away. Time was someone else's story. Only the afternoon for us, the air wide and breathless, the sea standing at ease.

I can remember the catches we made — and the clear pools we gazed in. Not for our own reflections were we staring. Our young unfinished faces were attentive. Look, the fish darting, the water clouding.

Everything was silent. A circle of silence. Sometimes the sea broke the circle. You could hear its crisp murmur, its hint of disasters. Not for us the hour of calamity.

Above was the cottage. The hammocks slung in trees for sleeping, the sure smoke from the chimney. The determined hour.

Love was far off — and passion. The milked cow, the fed chicken, the tired unhunting dogs — they were our setting.

I can remember sleep so deep that the sea seemed to enter it. Water washed on my window. I was curled in the shape of a seed, dreaming of being unborn.

But the morning was always there, over the window. Time was the sea slowing, the sand spreading, rocks drying and the cool wind breathing.

My world was the sea's edge, the warm breakers, the grey rocks. Distance was the Atlantic with huge convoys. I could not believe in the distance, though my gaze was as wide as the sky.

EXODUS

II

The wide emptiness of it: not snow in winter stretching the sky, not a dream breaking through a sleep and a sleep, but a calm safe place, a quiet place, a landscape.

(Children touch but never own. Children pick but never truly mutilate. Old men are made for madness and corruption. Yet only children can be truly cruel.)

Not whiteness here either, not harvest or snow or sunk sky or sea grown wilful. Simply the fields—and the child watching.

You could take air into your hands then, you could breathe and a word was assured. You could understand all taming yet never wish to capture. You could feel the world turning.

(Only the old are arrogant: what have they left but wishes? The old man at the corner grasps your money. The woman puts her hand against her breast. These beg for pity out of hopelessness.)

The child is anonymous, casual: his name surprises him. He is the air he breathes and earth he touches. Later the christening with the salt, the oils.

The harvest grows. He only sees the corn. The old man dies, his seed along with him. The child cannot penetrate the future: therefore he does not need or fear the past.

EXODUS

III

It was a night that nobody else knew: it was a wide breaking night. And the dreams came, deep and dark, places of blood and slaughter. Strange beasts slain but there was no executioner.

It was as if whiteness was taken away, as if when you looked for it, there was no place for whiteness, no room for it. Even the dead lacked their lilies.

My own shadow was strange to me — strange yet aware. Every sense had become painful. Everyone's gaze was inimical.

Yet I could recall, still, the cool corridors of childhood, the open delighted gardens, the body bare to the sun. Where was the sun-dial's shadow now? Would the sun never return?

Everything then was a looking, a gaze of candour. Eyes met fully, meaning a friendship. Body met body untouched by desire. Fear was over the wall, a ball flung by an unseen child, a shadow that crept up the stair.

I could remember it all, like somebody else's story, like somebody else's innocence. I was wholly aware now — trapped beast ready to flinch, fearful of touching or tasting.

And all this strangeness — the pain in the body, the child's flesh paling, the shadow grown wider — all this was a country I feared to discover. I would not believe it was mine.

Love was something else, nothing to do with this, no part in the stretching body, the blood leaping. Over the wall I could hear the whisper of lovers, a child crying across their voices. And hearing them — I was afraid.

EXODUS

IV

There are no white rooms now, no places where you can be seen and not recognised, no fields untrampled on. What will defend you now is all your own.

Can you relinquish the mood of childhood? Wholly resign the care, the urgent need? Dare you contract responsibilities? Who lives in white rooms now?

(So many are explorers. Children with sleds and dogs and fur-lined boots. Who needs to see the Pole or any star? What is there now to prove?)

On the edge of childhood, tilted towards maturity, on a grey world turning and a moon changing, I can be stable yet susceptible. I crave for causes now and lasting things.

I am English—and on the surface made of gentle moods. Yet long for south and sun, seek for the white cities, vines on walls, sea left where the sands mould it, flesh sun-burnt and surrendered.

(Can childhood be cast off on a coast? What seas will bear such flotsam? Can suffering surrender and survive?)

High now in Europe, with a window that shapes me a world—I am the child that gathered broken grasses, that dreamt and screamed across the night. Yet every gentle thing has stalwart roots. The sensitive survive and tell their story.

(Order is found, not imposed. Explorers find but do not legislate. Kings crumble with the ruins that they build. The young throw shadows which they have not earned. Our darkness is a promise of survival.)

The world is older than our steps across it. Yet who can bear the pressure of the past? Or move into the future unconcerned? We are no longer children, are full-grown.

Clumsy the climbers now, and bold explorers. We have more seasons than we care to name.

EXODUS

V

It is discovery without ownership, it is trading a word for a vision, it is touching without possession.

(Who understands his own ambition, dare anchor in a sense of his survival, pocket a life and let the profits pass? None is quite arrogant or sure enough.)

So we collect, pack drawers, put books on shelves, plant gardens with perennial flowers. Our seed becomes a son.

All for a reassurance. We dare not be quite feckless or quite wild. We fear the weather and the wind which scatters. Mostly our wishes are concerned with building.

(Where is the child now, the adolescent. We eat and change but still the flesh remains. I am the self I always was. Who fails to recognise himself in mirrors?)

We have grown apt at ballasting and softening. We know the power of palliatives. Have come to terms, it seems, with pain. Yet still we envy every child's delight. Our sleep is shallow and we fear to wake.

Books, bric-à-brac and *objets d'art*. Photographs of the past. The lovely summer when we fell in love. The church we prayed in and forgot ourselves. The open window and the unclaimed view—we cling to such and bring the wild birds down, yet cannot even guard the things we love.

RETORT TO THE ANTI-ABSTRACTIONISTS

The world had grown too complicated, so
He went back to the cause of things and laid
The fiery day within an early shade.
It was impossible to see things grow.

And this he knew and meant. Do not believe
This picture was achieved without much care.
The man drew dangerously toward despair,
Trying to show what inward eyes perceive.

The pattern now demands our firm attention,
But still spectators say, 'What does it mean?
This is not anything that I have seen.'
There is so much the painter could not mention.

His picture shows the meaning, not the things—
The look without the face, flight without wings.

THE CONFIDENCE

After that moment when at last you let
The whole thing out, the grievances, the fear,
Did you then find it all could disappear,
Clothed in the kindly words 'Forgive, forget'?

It was not so. You only felt the shame
Of being caught out in a hopeless hour,
Of being once again within men's power,
A pawn, a puppet in a grown-up game.

Yet if you loved them and if they loved you
Beyond the carefully chosen words, the wide
Disarming land where terror seemed to hide
But could not, would the older wish come true?

Would someone still be able to confess
That he was more than his unhappiness?

WARNING TO PARENTS

Save them from terror; do not let them see
The ghost behind the stairs, the hidden crime.
They will, no doubt, grow out of this in time
And be impervious as you and me.

Be sure there is a night-light close at hand;
The plot of that old film may well come back,
The ceiling, with its long, uneven crack,
May hint at things no child can understand.

You do all this and are surprised one day
When you discover how the child can gloat
On Belsen and on tortures — things remote
To him. You find it hard to watch him play

With thoughts like these, and find it harder still
To think back to the time when you also
Caught from the cruel past a childish glow
And felt along your veins the wish to kill.

Fears are more personal than we had guessed —
We only need ourselves; time does the rest.

HAPPY FAMILIES

The Strangers came and offered to stand in
For one of us still missing. So we dealt
The cards, and hoped that someone would begin.
Each hid what he imagined he had felt.

Oh, look how Mrs. Beef, how Master Bun
Step out and stare; someone has got the set.
We sit about, cards clutched, each one alone,
Wishing our blood, our minds had never met.

Someone upstairs is weeping on his bed
(Families can hurt much more than strangers do).
No one consoles; we take our cards instead,
Watching Miss Grit and Mr. Satin go.

But when the game is put away at last
And each goes quietly to his own room,
How many then will weep for some lost past
Or see a private shadow in the gloom?

DARKNESS

The water is troubled and the dark
Wind moves over it.
How do I know the wind is dark?
I only guess how the crowded world discovers my window,
How wild creatures, even in this city, stir
About their dark purposes.
And I too, unable now to be dark,
Unable now to be heavy
Under the sleep the pills will bring me,
Lie awake thinking—
'I can balance the world on my thought.'
Like the lips of a bowl where a flower is brooding,
I hold my fingers.
Wait, wait. Soon, softly
And darkly
A flower will come,
A creature will move
Out of the moss, the grass, the hole; the earth
Will discard it. Soon,
With flickering eyes (and the flowers with trembling petals),
It will wait for the world to discover it.

I am lying here and I wait
For the dark to open, for something whole to welcome
My staring eyes. A moth is beating about
The lamp. So many twitchings and stirrings.
I wish for some support of my sleeplessness,
For fingers around a bowl,
Someone, perhaps, just waiting.
I have pushed the earth aside, I am waiting, alert.

MAH JONG

Intricate pieces: children,
We could not understand them,
Played with them like bricks, built
On the card-table's soft felt,
A world, a city, then
You suddenly broke the dream.

We knew you as presence, a far
Mood, something close to war.
That evening, the cups on the dresser
Shook; my sister and I
Watched fear fall from the sky.

You carried away the game,
Offered it to our nurse.
We had lost, you said, the rules,
Both of us too young for schools
Or for parents' stratagem.
In bed we had nightmares.

THE STORM HOUSE

The wind is shaking this house,
This new house, nine storeys high and no one guessing
Such newness could ever be broached. The storm has done it,
The only natural sound in the whole city.

Along the river the boats are hooting farewell
And lights are coming on in the dingy streets.
Somebody, far-off, kicks a can and then
Returns to his separateness, his only gesture
Echoing down the street against the storm.

This moderate skyscraper is full of sickness,
A hospital houses a hundred different ailments.
The wind grows strong, winding a noisy bandage
Around the building; human sounds are unheard.

And if you cried, you would have to cry so loudly
That the wind was stilled a moment as if a hand,
In godlike supplication, laid peace upon it,
But the gods we invoke are quiet here as our prayers.

PROBLEMS OF VIEWING

I. THE OPEN CAPITAL

Smoke rises and houses emerge
In geometric squares.
It is a question of how much the eye can hold
As it stares, impossibly filling
Its small space with a crowd, a street,
A distant hill;
And then the sky (that is another problem).
One thing is clear:
Only a little can be taken away,
The view will break but will not give itself wholly.

I am speaking of looking.
There is no emotion,
No choice clouded by desire
As, say, when one sees a glass of water.
Here is a city smudged with smoke,
Stirring towards noon.
To look is to make a simple decision.

No one persuades you.
It is, perhaps, peculiarly human
To gaze upon this and, uncontemplative,
Hoarding the view for a further occasion, turn
To something that needs your touch, your arbitration.

II. THE UNFOLDING

It was the way
The eye opened on to it,
And then how all
The other four astonished senses came
To its assistance.

Say that the spring is late,
Say that we needed some attentive pause:
All these but add to a devoted spring.
That flower is pushing through the earth, I see,
And in an air that scarcely moves the skin,
Something is growing. Watch it how you will
(And use a whole night's vigil for the act),
Still you can never say the second when
The petals pushed to independent life.

III. TO PAINT THE DAWN

You will need more than a northern light for this:
You will need hard thick paint,
To give this strange light emphasis,
To suggest life and half-life.

Nothing human will help you
But your own breathing, your own calm.
All the power that holding a brush has ever
Brought you will surely be needed now; the view
Is moving away but still warm.

Before it goes, before it finally goes,
At least fill out the darkness with some brief
Positive clarity — the hint of a rose
Towering a moment, say, above its leaf.

IV. PROVISIONAL ATTEMPT

Daily the cars race past.
Seasons seem irrelevant where the traffic
Coasts so constantly. Flowers are dusty before
Their blossoming, and air
Is filled with petrol and smoke before it reaches
The nose. The hand is gritty, the eye unsure.

Somebody swiftly pulls a curtain back
And then you can see the street either as they
See it, expectantly, or else
Can force your eyes into that darkened room
Swarming with shadows, and train your tired vision
To choose and affirm the solid objects there.

ADMONITION

Watch carefully. These offer
Surprising statements, are not
Open to your proper doubt,
Will watch you while you suffer.

Sign nothing but let the vague
Slogans stand without your name.
Your indifference they claim
Though the issues seem so big.

Signing a paper puts off
Your responsibilities.
Trust rather your own distress
As in, say, matters of love.

Always behind you, judges
Will have something trite to say.
Let them know you want delay;
No star's smooth at its edges.

PARTS OF A ZODIAC

I. SCALES

Under this star they will expect always
A sense of balance, a calm which spreads
Out from your life to the world. You will
Find many coming to you for advice.
Heed emotion, offer few words,
Whatever you say will be repeated.
To yourself, perhaps, the balance will seem

Always precarious; nervous fingers
Will seem to thrust from every quarter
Swaying your sense of perfect justice.
Nor does this inborn balance denote
A lukewarm heart. Rather, you hide
All that might breach your detachment. You hold
The weights in your hand; only you can decide.

II. PISCES

From a sliding smooth element
These came and to this they return,
Fish-like bobbing to a word, a hint,
Then back, back, quick under the stern

Of somebody else's thought (borrowers these, ever)
And nothing but a smooth surface left. You would guess
Under this star is born The Deceiver;
Not so, simply a kind of shyness.

In this month, skies are not clear yet, stars
Uncertain, not easily seen; they swim
On their own mysterious adventures.
Those born under them know the same whim.

THE YOUNG ONES

They slip on to the bus, hair piled up high.
New styles each month, it seems to me. I look,
Not wanting to be seen, casting my eye
Above the unread pages of a book.

They are fifteen or so. When I was thus,
I huddled in school coats, my satchel hung
Lop-sided on my shoulder. Without fuss
These enter adolescence; being young

Seems good to them, a state we cannot reach,
No talk of 'awkward ages' now. I see
How childish gazes staring out of each
Unfinished face prove me incredibly

Old-fashioned. Yet at least I have the chance
To size up several stages — young yet old,
Doing the twist, mocking an 'old-time' dance:
So many ways to be unsure or bold.

A PICTURE

That dark one in the corner strokes his knife,
Knowing that he can use it if too much
Is asked of him, or if a sudden touch
Shocks him to new awarenesses of life.

The light surrounds the stronger one who fills
The middle distance. Is he thief or saint?
The artist here has shown a bold restraint,
Guessing the hint and not the climax kills.

There is a shadow that he could not find
The colour for. It haunts the picture and
Seems a deliberate gesture of the hand.
But no one saw inside the painter's mind.

THE SHELLS

I have the shells now in a leather box—
Limpets and cowries, ones like hands spread out.
Lifeless they are yet bear the weight of doubt
And of desire with all its hidden shocks.

Once, as a child, I might have pressed the shell
Close to my ear and thought I heard the sea.
Now I hear absence sighing quietly.
I am the one who makes and pulls the bell.

You gathered these and so they bear your print.
I cannot see it, yet the simply knowing
That you have marked these shells keeps my love growing.
Passion can hide in any lifeless hint.

A sentiment perhaps, yet every gift
Carries the weight of all we did not do.
The shells are fragments and the fragments few,
But you still sound in what the shells have left.

THE DESTROYERS

There was a little damage done that day.
A few bricks crumbled and a few men said
Words at the worst to kill, at best betray.

There was no violence, no sudden dead
Strewn in the streets. Things simply wore away.
Where once were houses, there were stones instead

There was discomfort everywhere, no one
Felt quite at ease. Even the madmen stirred
In their cold beds. Some evil had been done.

And yet the journals scarcely hold a word
Of crucial pain, disaster or decay.
No one has spoken though they all have heard.

We gaze at one another now afraid
Of what we think, of what we long to love.
Handshakes, like kisses, also have betrayed.

Later there will be sacrifice enough.
Can nothing now be done to cause delay?
Within myself the slow destroyers move.

How do they work? What is it that they say?

A GAME OF CARDS

Determined to be peaceful, we played cards,
Dealt out the hands and hid from one another
Our power. Our only words were weightless words
Like 'Your turn', 'Thank you' — words to soothe and smother;
Our pulses, slowed to softness, moved together.

So we became opponents and could stare
Like strangers, guessing what the other held.
There was no look of love or passion there.
The pasteboard figures sheltered us, compelled
Each one to win. Love was another world.

And yet within the concentration which
Held us so fast, some tenderness slipped in,
Some subtle feeling which could deftly breach
The kings and queens and prove the pasteboard thin:
Another battle thundered to begin.

A NEW PAIN

When you have gone, I sit and wait, diminished
More than I ever was when quite alone.
Where nothing started, nothing need be finished;
Something of love I learn when you have gone,

Something I never knew before; I mean
The ache, the rending and the dispossession.
When I was quite alone I felt no keen
Edge of the blade, the other side of passion.

Absence becomes almost a presence since
It casts so deep a shadow on my mind:
No trivial lights will comfort or convince,
I lack your way of looking and am blind.

But when you come expectedly, it is
As if more absences than one were cast
Into oblivion. Present ecstasies
Thrive on the very anguish of the past.

THE MIND HAS MOUNTAINS

1966

IN A MENTAL HOSPITAL SITTING-ROOM

Utrillo on the wall. A nun is climbing
Steps in Montmartre. We patients sit below.
It does not seem a time for lucid rhyming;
Too much disturbs. It does not seem a time
When anything could fertilize or grow.

It is as if a scream were opened wide,
A mouth demanding everyone to listen.
Too many people cry, too many hide
And stare into themselves. I am afraid.
There are no life-belts here on which to fasten.

The nun is climbing up those steps. The room
Shifts till the dust flies in between our eyes.
The only hope is visitors will come
And talk of other things than our disease ...
So much is stagnant and yet nothing dies.

DIAGNOSIS AND PROTEST

To be surprised because someone is kind,
To fear to walk into a room and find

Stares of hostility, to try to please
By giving presents, saying 'My fault', — these

Have been my lifelong habits, and I'm told
Now that they are a sign I have not grown

In many ways, that part of me — emotion —
Is infantile. And yet I have known passion,

Wanted requited love, desired a child.
Perhaps if I were wholly undefiled

(Too strong a word and yet not wholly false)
I would not feel these conflicts now. Such ills

(And that is what they're called) can yet produce
A vivid work of art. But who would choose —

If this *must* be the price — such childlike pain?
I think the answer is we cannot learn

Completely to be bitter; if we did,
Whatever art we practise would be dead.

Maybe for me it's necessary to
Feel guilt always. I love the scapegoat so,

Also the clown — by Chaplin or Rouault.

MADNESS

Then this is being mad; there is no more
Imagining, Ophelias of the mind.
This girl who shouts and slobbers on the floor,
Sending us frightened to the corner, is
To all the world we know now deaf and blind
And we are merely loathsome enemies.

It is the lack of reason makes us fear,
The feeling that ourselves might be like this.
We are afraid to help her or draw near
As if she were infectious and could give
Some taint, some touch of her own fantasies,
Destroying all the things for which we live.

And, worse than this, we hate the madness too
And hate the mad one. Measured off a space
There is a world where things run calm and true—
But not for us. We have to be with her
Because our minds are also out of place
And we have carried more than we can bear.

REFLECTIONS ON A MENTAL HOSPITAL

'A pretty flower,' one says. No answers come;
A nurse turns out the helpless visitors.
Silence at last seeps slowly through the room.
One in a corner, deeply drugged, just stirs
And screens are brought; no-one

Must see the tossing, though they are allowed
To hear the sounds and build from them a whole
Body of pain and hopelessness. Aloud,
One getting well, says 'I can't bear it all',
But does and grows less proud;

Because she knows how near an edge it is
To cast out reason, lie beneath the sheets
Abandoning oneself to kindnesses
One has, perhaps, no right to. A nerve beats
Harsh in these heads. What is

The quick of sicknesses that run like this?
I never thought I would be cast among
The textbook symptoms and the illnesses
That cannot be defined. I feel too young
To be locked up with these.

Little is known about the human brain.
This is the truth. All is empirical:
Oh is the horoscope come back again,
Or are we reaching back but to the Fall,
The fruit, the grasp, the pain?

THE INTERROGATOR

He is always right.
However you prevaricate or question his motives,
Whatever you say to excuse yourself
He is always right.

He always has an answer;
It may be a question that hurts to hear.
It may be a sentence that makes you flinch.
He always has an answer.

He always knows best.
He can tell you why you disliked your father,
He can make your purest motive seem aggressive.
He always knows best.

He can always find words.
While you fumble to feel for your own position
Or stammer out words that are not quite accurate,
He can always find words.

And if you accuse him
He is glad you have lost your temper with him.
He can find the motive, give you a reason
If you accuse him.

And if you covered his mouth with your hand,
Pinned him down to his smooth desk chair,
You would be doing just what he wishes.
His silence would prove that he was right.

VAN GOGH

All your best paintings, I have heard, were made
When you were mad. I know you sliced your ear
Off, went insane. Yet only that church in
The Louvre might possibly suggest you had
Something that most men call a mental flaw;
Yet even there's a woman with a thin

Bonnet and skirts raised from the dusty ground.
Detail you saw, and foolish men suggest
Such probing gazes are a sign of being
A little crazy, not quite balanced, found,
When tested, passionate, too much depressed,
Quickly in tears. This was your way of seeing.

There is a theory that the very heart
Of making means a flaw, neurosis, some
Sickness; yet others say it is release.
I only know that your wild, surging art
Took you to agony, but makes us come
Strangely to gentleness, a sense of peace.

THE JUMP

They say there was no plan. Why are they sure?
Apparently the police have evidence.
One clue they think is that she had with her
New clothes, just bought. Now, who would lay their plans

For death, and then go in a shop and buy
An anorak and shoes? Yes, they insist
That human beings who elect to die
Do not behave with such a curious twist.

Oh certainly she jumped, but everyone—
Doctors and police—says that the impulse came
In one split second. Down below, the town
Must have looked ordinary, just the same

As any Friday afternoon. I think
That no-one knows how long she had thought over
Committing suicide; she saw the brink,
The dark .... That day I'd helped her with the Hoover.

ATTEMPTED SUICIDES

We have come back.
Do not be surprised if we blink our eyes
If we stare oddly
If we hide in corners.
It is we, not you, who should show surprise.

For everything looks strange.
Roofs are made of paper
Hands are muslin
Babies look eatable.
There has been too much change.

And where do we come from?
Where did the pills take us,
The gas,
The water left pouring?
Limbo? Hell? Mere forgetfulness?

It was a lost moment,
There were no dreams,
There was simply the beyond-endurance
And then the coming-to
To you and you and you and you.

Do not ask us,
As if we were Lazarus,
What it was like.
We never got far enough.
Now we touch ourselves and feel strange.
We have a whole world to arrange.

LISA

'You don't like being touched,' she said, that kid
Of only fifteen. She was very quick,
Very mature in some things that she said;
At others, certainly unstable, sick.

Like most of us, she was disturbed, distressed,
And yet she had a natural touch with things
Like toys and children. She was not depressed,
Only quite lost among her sufferings.

I liked her very much and she liked me,
She taught me much, I know. But I taught her
Only how little age and family
Matter when one has loved in terms of fear.

QUESTIONS

You have said
Over and over again
You are only there to help,
I must grow the grain,
Break down, break down,
Then build up again.

But what are these talks doing?
And these silences?
Something in me holds on to personalities;
Are you really destroying
What I need and love?
I speak through a veil of incoherences.
You never move.

I have done
The ultimate thing,
Tried death and was brought back,
Played at Judas but not known
That someone would turn off the gas—
The one who has grown
Close into lovelessness.
We are tied together now on a rack.

But only I have to learn
Childhood, sex, love
All over again.
He is too old, has moved off.
Yet I, his seed
Have come closer to death,
And further, perhaps, than his need.

NIGHT SISTER

How is it possible not to grow hard,
To build a shell around yourself when you
Have to watch so much pain, and hear it too?
Many you see are puzzled, wounded; few
Are cheerful long. How can you not be scarred?

To view a birth or death seems natural,
But these locked doors, these sudden shouts and tears
Graze all the peaceful skies. A world of fears
Like the ghost-haunting of the owl appears.
And yet you love that stillness and that call.

You have a memory for everyone;
None is anonymous and so you cure
What few with such compassion could endure.
I never met a calling quite so pure.
My fears are silenced by the things you've done.

We have grown cynical and often miss
The perfect thing. Embarrassment also
Convinces us we cannot dare to show
Our sickness. But you listen and we know
That you can meet us in our own distress.

THE ILLUSION

The sun, a child at play, and one or two
Young people lying on the lawn, a place
That seems so peaceful that they can't be true,
Those horrors, and so much unhappiness.

Much is the same as what we know outside—
People hold hands here, others sit apart.
A casual glance could never quite divide
The normal from the sick and frightened heart.

Oddly, it's *here* I learn, with fear and pain
Rooted within myself, new words, new tongues,
New honesties and courage that sustain
The power to bear what man has made of things.

Only one horror haunts and lives with me
And won't be shed. I have learnt here also,
In one long look of naked cruelty,
How man can dream of Belsen, make it grow.

HYSTERIA

It was at breakfast only yesterday
(Patients, like children, gobbling porridge up),
That suddenly this loud inhuman voice
Broke through the semi-peace, the childish noise.
A few of us crashed down a spoon or cup,
But all, I think, willed her to go away.

Not only what is just irrational
Infected us. It was the staring eyes,
The knowledge, too, how close all people are
To what is meaningless. Hysteria
Is like a zoo where each wild creature lies
Ready to pounce, not wanting man's control.

Yet at the end of all this shrieking came
The whimper, 'I regret the things I do.'
Most of us were too shaken then to try
And treat her like a baby who must cry,
Although we do not guess the cause.
I envy those who've learnt what they must do
Though honest nurses say they too feel shame.

WORDS FROM TRAHERNE

'You cannot love too much, only in the wrong way.'

It seemed like love; there were so many ways
Of feeling, thinking, each quite separate.
Tempers would rise up in a sudden blaze,
Or someone coming twitch and shake the heart.

Simply, there was no calm. Fear often came
And intervened between the quick expression
Of honest movements or a kind of game.
I ran away at any chance of passion.

But not for long. Few can avoid emotion
So powerful, although it terrifies
I trembled, yet I wanted that commotion
Learnt through the hand, the lips, the ears, the eyes.

Fear always stopped my every wish to give.
I opted out, broke hearts, but most of all
I broke my own. I would not let it live
Lest it should make me lose control and fall.

Now generosity, integrity,
Compassion too, are what make me exist,
Yet still I cannot come to terms or try,
Or even know, the knot I must untwist.

A NURSE GONE SICK

You cared for us and now I hear that you
Are sick. I sometimes guessed at it perhaps.
There were those days when you seemed near to tears
As if you could not bear the trials and traps
Of nursing those whose minds have gone askew.
They seemed too much for you — our pains and fears.

And once I said in secret to a friend
'She understands since she has suffered too.'
Odd that I should so nearly comprehend
Yet learn your pain the wrong way round. For you
Had come not to a starting but an end.
Now I regret that far too late I knew.

FINAL CONSIDERATIONS

The bottle or the needle or the gas;
More choose the pill. They leave themselves a chance
Of getting back. Others grip hopelessness.
But why was no-one there with some defence
That might have shown despair as something less

Than their thin world—within, without? I too
Know what it means to want to reach the end,
Have made attempts. There seemed no need of friend
Or hope of future. Terror simply drew
Me on to dark I did not understand;
I did not know then what I wished to do.

Oh, Judas hanging on a tree was close
To Christ in time; in pain perhaps also.
He had the chance to make his peace, God knows,
But only God knows why he had to go
Swinging upon the rope. Men suffer so;
I am with them now who revived but chose.

SAMUEL PALMER AND CHAGALL

You would have understood each other well
And proved to us how periods of art
Are less important than the personal
Worlds that each painter makes from mind and heart.

The greatest — Blake, Picasso — move about
In many worlds. *You* only have one small
Yet perfect place. In it, there is no doubt,
And no deception can exist at all.

Great qualities make such art possible,
A sense of TRUTH, integrity, a view
Of man that fits into a world that's whole,
Those moons, those marriages, that dark, that blue.

I feel a quiet in it all although
The subject and the scenes are always strange.
I think it is that order pushes through
Your images, and so you can arrange

And make the wildest, darkest dream serene;
Landscapes are like still-lives which somehow move,
The moon and sun shine out of the same scene —
Fantastic worlds but all are built from love.

ON A FRIEND'S RELAPSE AND RETURN TO A MENTAL CLINIC

I had a feeling that you might come back,
And dreaded it.
You are a friend, your absence is a lack;
I mean now that

We do not meet outside the hospital:
You are too ill
And I, though free by day, cannot yet call
Myself quite well.

Because of all of this, it was a shock
To find that you
Were really bad, depressed, withdrawn from me
More than I knew.

You ask for me and sometimes I'm allowed
To go and sit
And gently talk to you — no noise too loud:
I'm glad of it.

You take my hand, say odd things, sometimes weep,
And I return
With rational talk until you fall asleep.
So much to learn

Here; there's no end either at second-hand
Or else within
Oneself, or both. I want to understand
But just begin

When something startling, wounding comes again.
Oh heal my friend.
There should be peace for gentle ones, not pain.
Bring her an end

Of suffering, or let us all protest
And realize
It is the good who often know joy least.
I fight against the size

And weight of such a realization, would
Prefer no answers trite
As this; but feeling that I've understood,
I can accept, not fight.

OLD AGE

You were quite silent till the doctor came
Kindly to question, breaking through your thoughts.
And were you glad that he recalled your name,
  Asked you about your pets,
Or would you rather doze there, much the same

As some old cat or dog, some lump of fur
Beside the fire, unmoving and unmoved,
Grateful that no-one made you speak or stir,
  Yet wanting to be loved
And finding it in warm sheets and soft chair?

You know who gives real kindness, none the less,
Not to child's shouting like some old ones do.
You feel for certain hands as though to bless,
  And beg a blessing too;
And then you weep, simply from happiness.

NIGHT GARDEN OF THE ASYLUM

An owl's call scrapes the stillness.
Curtains are barriers and behind them
The beds settle into neat rows.
Soon they'll be ruffled.

The garden knows nothing of illness.
Only it knows of the slow gleam
Of stars, the moon's distilling; it knows
Why the beds and lawns are levelled.

Then all is broken from its fullness.
A human cry cuts across a dream.
A wild hand squeezes an open rose.
We are in witchcraft, bedevilled.

A BABY BORN IN HOSPITAL

FOR M.

One normal voice — a child's across the night.
Its sleep is broken by some natural need.
The corridor is blazing with a light
But he screams in the darkness, wants to feed.

Out of the mother's anguished pain he came,
Fragile to touch and strangely beautiful.
He smiles and thrusts his finger out to claim
Each being here — the sick, the getting well.

From parents wishing perfect love, he grew
And lives with us in innocent compassion.
Will some rare pity linger in him too
When out of childhood? A dream, a vision?

But yet to mother and to child I wish
Oblivion of all they have known here.
Love wrought this wonder from the simple flesh
Where no pain need be and no grief to bear.

PERSONAL EASTER

Let them bring gifts, let them bring pious eggs.
There are no kings at Easter, only men.
Two nights ago, we drained cups to the dregs
And did not know if we should live again.
The stars move on, we battle with our plagues.
What god will rise now from the frozen stone?

A few flowers sprinkle over ravaged earth.
Birds hover, dive. Why do they fill my mind?
The Holy Ghost has more august a birth
Than this, the tongues of fire could singe and blind.
Oh God, last year I chose my own poor death
Yet you arose me, left Limbo behind.

A DEPRESSION

She left the room undusted, did not care
To hang a picture, even lay a book
On the small table. All her pain was there—
In absences. The furious window shook
With violent storms she had no power to share.

Her face was lined, her bones stood thinly out.
She spoke, it's true, but not as if it mattered;
She helped with washing-up and things like that.
Her face looked anguished when the china clattered.
Mostly she merely stared at us and sat.

And then one day quite suddenly she came
Back to the world where flowers and pictures grow
(We sensed that world though we were much the same
As her). She seemed to have the power to know
And care and treat the whole thing as a game.

But will it last? Those prints upon her walls,
Those stacks of books—will they soon disappear?
I do not know how a depression falls
Or why so many of us live in fear.
The cure, as much as the disease, appals.

GROVE HOUSE, IFFLEY

FOR VIVIEN

Your house is full of objects that I prize—
A marble hand, paperweights that uncurl,
Unfolding endlessly to red or blue.
Each way I look, some loved thing meets my eyes,
And you have used the light outside also;
The autumn gilds collections old and new.

And yet there is no sense of *objets d'art*,
Of rarities just valued for their worth.
The handsome objects here invite one's touch,
As well as sight. Without the human heart,
They'd have no value, would not say so much.
Something of death belongs to them—and birth.

Nor are they an escape for anyone.
Simply you've fashioned somewhere that can give
Not titillation, pleasure, but a sense
Of order and of being loved; you've done
What few can do who bear the scars and prints
Of wounds from which they've learnt a way to live.

SUICIDES

(FOR A PSYCHIATRIST)

I wish that I could help you when this happens,
When patients you have tended seek their end.
It does not matter what the way, the weapons.
What does it feel like? How can you pretend

All is the same, that something merely failed?
How do you know that a chance word of yours
May have affected them until they willed
To die, and made you the unwilling cause?

Stupid and childish now, I want to cry
To think of threats that I have made to you.
I've said, 'You would not worry if I die.'
It is not true: I know it is not true.

You take on more than many other men —
The quick and sick of life. I wish I knew
How I could help. But I have also been,
And am, your burden and your thread of pain.

CARAVAGGIO'S 'NARCISSUS' IN ROME

Look at yourself, the shine, the sheer
Embodiment thrown back in some
Medium like wood or glass. You stare,
And many to this gallery come
Simply to see this picture. Clear
As glass it is. It holds the eye
By subject and by symmetry.

Yes, something of yourself is said
In this great shining figure. You
Must have come to self-knowledge, read
Yourself within that image who
Draws every visitor. You made
From gleaming paint that tempting thing—
Man staring at his suffering.

And at his joy. But you stopped where
We cannot pause, merely make sure
The picture took you from the stare,
Fatal within: Chagall or Blake
Have exorcized your gazing for
A meaning that you could not find
In the cold searchings of your mind.

CHINESE ART

You said you did not care for Chinese art
Because you could not tell what dynasty
A scroll or bowl came from. 'There is no heart'
You said, 'Where time's avoided consciously.'

I saw your point because I loved you then.
The willows and the horses and the birds
Seemed cold to me; each skilfully laid-on, thin
Phrase spoke like nothing but unpassionate words.

I understand now what those artists meant;
They did not care for style at all, or fashion.
It was eternity they tried to paint,
And timelessness, they thought, must lack all passion.

Odd that just when my feeling need for you
Has gone all wrong, I should discover this.
Yes, but I lack the sense of what is true
Within these wise old artists' skilfulness.

It would be easy now to close again
My heart against such hurt. Those willows show,
In one quick stroke, a lover feeling pain,
And birds escape fast as the brush-strokes go.

LATE CHILD

FOR L. L.

If many children had been born to them,
They would have seen, after the first delight,
Another note being added to the theme —
A pleasure and a joy — sometimes a fright.

But you have made yourselves more vulnerable,
Put at the mercy of such ecstasy;
Everything that this baby does you feel
As a new wonder, nothing is casually

Observed or, let alone, taken for granted.
The sperm, the seed, the blood, the milk — all these
Are something that you passionately wanted;
All are embodied in the child you praise.

Few are as innocent or glad as this.
This child come to a childless pair has made
Me think of times before the serpent's hiss.
Yet I am frightened too, since this delayed

Daughter means everything. What if she died?
Or if some sickness ruined all she seems
To be (so perfect now)? You have defied
Disaster, living only in your dreams.

I think I know a little what you feel,
Being myself childless a different way.
When I see babies, they are not quite real.
I know, like you, the wonder — and dismay.

LOVE POEM

There is a shyness that we have
Only with those whom we most love.
Something it has to do also
With how we cannot bring to mind
A face whose every line we know.
O love is kind, O love is kind.

That there should still remain the first
Sweetness, also the later thirst—
This is why pain must play some part
In all true feelings that we find
And every shaking of the heart.
O love is kind, O love is kind.

And it is right that we should want
Discretion, secrecy, no hint
Of what we share. Love which cries out,
And wants the world to understand,
Is love that holds itself in doubt.
For love is quiet, and love is kind.

ONE FLESH

Lying apart now, each in a separate bed,
He with a book, keeping the light on late,
She like a girl dreaming of childhood,
All men elsewhere — it is as if they wait
Some new event: the book he holds unread,
Her eyes fixed on the shadows overhead.

Tossed up like flotsam from a former passion,
How cool they lie. They hardly ever touch,
Or if they do it is like a confession
Of having little feeling — or too much.
Chastity faces them, a destination
For which their whole lives were a preparation.

Strangely apart, yet strangely close together,
Silence between them like a thread to hold
And not wind in. And time itself's a feather
Touching them gently. Do they know they're old,
These two who are my father and my mother
Whose fire from which I came, has now grown cold?

THINKING OF LOVE

That desire is quite over
Or seems so as I lie
Using the sky as cover
And thinking of deep
Dreams unknown to a lover.

Being alone is now
Far from loneliness.
I can stretch and allow
Legs, arms, hands
Their complete freedom:
There is no-one to please.

But soon it comes —
Not simply the ache
Of a particular need,
But also the general hunger,
As if the flesh were a house
With too many empty rooms.

VAN GOGH AGAIN

This place is too mild,
Nothing dangerous could
Happen here, I think:
Nothing great, either.
If somebody screams or throws
A tea-cup through a window,
They are removed elsewhere.

It is chastening to reflect
That had Van Gogh been brought
(By accident, of course)
Into this mild ward,
And gone berserk one night
In the middle of painting,
Oh, say, the moonlight,

He would soon have gone
To a more hectic place,
And there, no doubt, have entered
A remote, fearful calm
Where everything was clear,
And, searching for something to do,
Would then have struck off his ear.

A BIRTHDAY IN HOSPITAL

(WRITTEN ON THE DAY)

Soon I shall be in tears this birthday morning:
Cards are propped up beside me, people come
And wish me happy days. In ceremony
(Even of childish sorts), I can behave,
Look interested, grateful, courteous,
Be to each one who comes a kind of warmth
And so give back not gratitude, but gifts.

Yet I shall cry, no doubt from loneliness,
From being far away from those I love,
Or any reason I can conjure later.
But are the tears themselves, I wonder, still
A sort of ceremony I must follow,
A childish ritual, necessity,
Something expected by the wishers-well?
I've heard of 'gift of tears' but did not know,
Until this moment, what the words could mean.

NEW POEM SIMPLY

Orwell invented the idea of a machine which makes novels
ten years ago my friends and I met
for group writing
it was a bit like Consequences
we took a subject
wrote a line
turned down the paper
passed it on
sometimes we got a real poem
but it was a hazard
(who said the so-called conventional poem isn't a hazard
anyway? and *what* is 'inspiration'?)
Our group worked better though at prose
it must be admitted
and when we had had a certain amount of rough wine

i am aware of the conventionality of all this
and of writing about it
What I really want
is a new kind of art altogether
trade all tradition
make music stand still
buildings be mobile
and everyone say (and mean it)
'How beautiful!'

and burn
you are a kind of flower
I worship you flowers
you are white in churches
and I have lighted you for prayers
in Barcelona they make wax legs wax babies
as thank-offerings
 blue candles
  you are not poetic
   not like the sea or the moon
    (i have not lighted you yet —
     i am holding my breath against the draught)

    children, light your sparklers
    blue will come at the end
    and the smell of burning
    Rembrandt you knew about light
    i'm putting the candles back in the box
    maybe i'll light them at Christmas
        blue, blue, blue

MY ROOM

it is full of things from my childhood
oh anyone could analyse it
but to paint it
that would be harder
it is mine yet not mine
Bonnard might have had a shot at it
dear Van Gogh — he would have had a go
and made it just like his own!
Vermeer? he'd have been concerned with mirrors:
and Picasso? it depends what period he was in
and what mood.

I have two rooms
the other is not so important
but it's full of my things
only the other day i dreamt that someone had come in
and smashed my treasures —
china, pots, wood, *papier maché,* books
the nightmare seemed to go on and on for hours

sometimes I want to clear everything out
except a table, a chair, a typewriter
but I know what would happen
first I'd try to make a mural
then books would appear
then papers
toys
bits and pieces from friends and holidays
and one enormous mirror, in which to stare.

this is my nursery and I like it.

it is my growing-up room also.

TREES

trees
  and the blowing through them
wind storm rain gale
oak ash sycamore beech
we cannot stand back and admire you long
not like the Roman pines
part of history
erect in the Forum
silent under the sun
layer on layer—
emperor, Pope, fascist, communist
and the trees still standing
in the churches you can munch God's bread
at any moment of the morning:
outside the Vespas race through Constantine's arch.

want a drink?
in the Via Veneto?
very good, *molto caro*? the Cafe Greco
or a Bloody Mary in the Via Condotti?
(oh stop showing off and talking like guide-books
everyone's been abroad now anyway)
why on earth should we feel proud that we've been to Ravenna or
    Florence?
it only needs money and perhaps a certain judgement.

Let's go to Brighton or Blackpool instead
Let's sleep in cold rooms with a single bed
bed and breakfast—what's wrong with that?
only it's likely to make you grow fat.
pink rock, fruit machines, 'what the butler saw'
we won't go to Paris or Rome any more
we'll pick up the shells as the rain falls down
or carry our boredom all round the town.

and what's the point of this?
it's only another affectation.

Romanesque
Gothic
Baroque—
why pretend they haven't got something
anyway, if you don't like history, you always get the sun abroad;
Casinos are more fun than bingo

but we were talking of trees . . .

JUST ANOTHER POEM

Words
stop it
you talk too much
words words words
Hamlet—
where do they get you
this sort of thing is old hat
anyway
(why 'hat'? Stop asking questions.)
don't censor it, just let the words flow she said
(this girl lies on a couch)
what about Joyce
and *Finnegans Wake*
and the end of *Ulysses*?
The funny thing is that Virginia Woolf
('Who's afraid of . . .' Don't *do* that)
got the feeling of stream of consciousness
by the most delicate writing in the world
poor thing, look what happened to her
it was all too much—
words and tears and war.
she was afraid even of reviews in *Granta*
all right, I know I'm involved in this
who says I shouldn't care anyway?

they say 'don't think about it'
I tell you I can't stop—at times that is

Hart Crane jumped into the sea
they covered up the reason
too many people are dying and unhappy

(when you mean what you say why does it sound like a cliché?)
what's God doing?
don't be blasphemous
the great big fathers are throwing rocks at you
but the Holy Ghost is settling down to sleep

UNKIND POEM ABOUT PEOPLE WHO ARE MILDLY DERANGED

i'm ill   I want psychoanalysis
i want oblivion
i want pills
'what's the matter with that woman?' ('don't speak so loudly')
'i don't care if she does hear'
'i slit my wrists you know: life was too much to bear
it gave my husband a shock all right'
they take away your money mirror and nail file
the lavatory doors won't lock
'would you like to go to the toilet dear' a nurse said
well '*toilet*': I mean to say

if anyone cries the others don't take the slightest notice
one keeps on about her operations
gall bladder
ulcers
tonsillitis
and *of course*
hysterectomy

some keep on about sex
'i can't bear my husband to touch me; it's "the change" you know'
give me the beatniks
with their jeans long hair drugs and dirt.

there are a few gentle ones who never talk about themselves
at times there are tears on their cheeks
they would give anything to hide them
other people's grief upsets them too;
odd what a touch on the wrist can do—
nurse's or patient's.

at times, I confess, I've thought there was nothing wrong with most of us

then why do we do what we do?

A LIMERICK AND SO ON

at Chartres the masons made
a church within the shade
they didn't claim
to sign their name—
the place was where you prayed.

God bless everyone
(are you being coy by any chance?)
i'm serious
you can't *try* to be simple
you either are or you're not
those men at Chartres were
so is Picasso
grinning as he finishes a plate

POEM ABOUT THE BREAKDOWN OF A BREAKDOWN

even the psycho admits it
        they don't know much about the human brain
poets know it is very delicate—
        hit it and the brains and blood will pour out like egg yolk.

what is the couch for then?
to protect this poor head
        to hide the psycho's perplexity from you?
        or make you feel like a baby again?
        Ring-a, ring-a-roses
        Freud is picking posies
        Guess what he will use them for?
        To make a sexual metaphor.

this poem is giving itself away too much

Hi Jung
How are you getting along?

Pity you didn't like trinities or triangles
that makes you a square
but still, Freud is top of the Hit Parade
heard his latest?
no but I can guess it's the old boy-meets-girl stuff

Adam sat under the magic tree
    Eve came up and kissed him
Oh Adam my darling one said she
    Get that bright apple down for me
    God isn't looking now, you see,
And anyway he was teasing us
When about *this* tree he made such a fuss

Adam looked up at the bough above
  And said, 'All right, let's do it.
God keeps talking to us of love
  This garden itself was made to prove
  Our life is simple, a shady grove,
Our lovely bodies.' Then why did they steal
  Apart when they'd eaten the fruit and feel
Something had disappeared — a game?
Or God himself? and feel such shame?

ever since we have been trying to get
  back to that garden
  Christ had to go, alone, to another one
  this poem has slipped away in the usual manner —
  Oh the bright apple-trees and skyscrapers.

SEA

                i'll have a go at it
some things are felt more if not mentioned
but that blue bloody sea
is too powerful
  i'm not going to mention the moon
or tides or anything like that
  i think of sex
    and the great urges
    and then of a child
(the only true picture Dali painted)—
'a child lifting the edge of the sea'
  he called it
    he's a smooth operator
      he even had to be clever about the crucifixion
        but something about the sea got him
          it's got me too
          always always:
          classical yet moving—

      there just aren't any words

THE SONNETS OF MICHELANGELO

1961

II

ON DANTE ALIGHIERI

It is not possible to say how much
We owe to him, because his splendour blinds
Our eyes. Simpler it is to blame those minds
Too small to honour him, to sense his touch.

He did not fear to plumb to places where
Failure alone survives. But this was done
For our example. Always he was near
To God. Only his country dared to shun

His greatness. Her ingratitude at last
Turned on herself. As proof of this, observe
How always to the perfect sorrows fall

Most painfully. To those who are the best
Most ill occurs. Dante did not deserve
Exile; his equal never lived at all.

III

TO POPE JULIUS II

My Lord, of all the ancient proverbs, this
Is surely true — 'Who *can* doth never will'.
You have believed in saws and promises
And blest those men whom falsehoods, not truths, fill.

Always I have been faithful and would give
Honour to you as rays do to the sun.
Yet all my pain has never made you grieve,
The less I please, the more work I have done.

Once I had hoped to climb by means of your
Great height, but now I find we rather need
Justice and power, not echoes faint indeed.

Heaven, it appears, itself is made impure
When worldliness has power. I live to take
Fruit from a tree too dry to bear or break.

VII

TO LUIGI DEL RICCIO

It happens sometimes even in the great
Sweetness of courtesy, of life and honour,
That an offence can hide. Thus, in this manner
Some good is spoilt and mars my healthy state.

He who can give to others wings of hope
Yet stretch a hidden net along their way,
Is false to the great fire of charity
And brings true friendship to a sudden stop.

Therefore, keep clear, Luigi, that first grace
To which I owe my life, let no storm mar
Its calm, let no wind stir its steady peace.

Contempt can make all gratitude obscure,
But, with true friendship, nothing can displace
Its strength. For this, pain is a way to please.

VIII

TO LUIGI DEL RICCIO
AFTER THE DEATH OF CECCHINO BRACCI

I scarcely knew him when his eyes were shut
For ever, he who was your life and light.
His eyes closed fast at death's last parting, but
Opened on God and found a love more bright.

I know and weep; yet it was not my fault
That I should meet him too late to admire
His grace. Your memory becomes his vault,
Lost not to you, only to my desire.

Then if, Luigi, I must carve the form
Of him, Cecchino, whom I speak about,
And change him from this dust to living stone,

You, his friend, must keep his image warm,
And if you fail, my art is called in doubt.
I'll find his likeness now in you alone.

X

TO GANDOLFO PORRINO
ON HIS MISTRESS FAUSTINA MANCINA

Unique in heaven as on this wicked earth
(Though cheaply by the vulgar crowd is she
Named — that crowd, too blind to see her worth),
The new high beauty was designed to be

For you alone. Neither with tools nor pen
Would I know how to fashion her or trace
The radiant beauty of her living face.
For that, you must return to life again.

And if she overwhelms imagination
As the great sun outshines the other stars,
Still you may rate her at her real price.

To calm your pining and your desolation
God moulds her beauty which can far surpass
All I can make. My art will not suffice.

XI

TO GIORGIO VASARI ON 'THE LIVES OF THE PAINTERS'

With pen and colours you have shown how art
Can equal nature. Also in a sense
You have from nature snatched her eminence,
Making the painted beauty touch the heart.

Now a more worthy work your skilful hand,
Writing on paper, labours and contrives—
To give to those who're dead new worth, new lives;
Where nature simply made, you understand.

When men have tried in other centuries
To vie with nature in the power to make,
Always they had to yield to her at last.

But you, illuminating memories,
Bring back to life these lives for their own sake,
And conquer nature with the vivid past.

XIII

TO THE SAME

To be more worthy of you, Lady, is
My sole desire. For all your kindnesses
I try to show, with all I have of art,
And courtesy, the gladness of my heart.

But well I know that simply by my own
Efforts I cannot match your goodness. Then
I ask you pardon for what's left undone,
And failing thus, I grow more wise again.

Indeed, I know it would be wrong to hope
That favours, raining from you as from heaven,
Could be repaid by human work so frail.

Art, talent, memory, with all their scope
Can never pay you back what you have given.
At this, a thousand tries would always fail.

XVI

Just as in pen and ink, the high and low
And mediocre styles can find expression,
And as in marbles the imagination,
Noble or base, will its own worth bestow;

So, my dear Lord, whatever finds its place
Within your heart — pride or humility —
I draw from it only what moves in me,
As you can tell from what shows on my face.

For he who sows both sighs and tears will find
(Since heaven, whose dew is always pure and clear,
To different seeds will variously appear),

That what he reaps is sorrow. Heart and mind,
When grievously afflicted, still will see
In greatest beauty only misery.

XVII

Lady, how can it be that what is shown
Through long experience and imagination
Endures so long in hard and mountain stone,
While years enact the maker's consummation?

The cause to the effect yields and gives place,
Nature by art is overcome at last.
I know too well who work with sculptor's grace
That time and death resign me to the past.

Thus can I give long life to you and me
In one way, either in stone or else in paint
Which seems to show each other's faces true.

Thus, in a thousand years all men shall see
How beautiful you were, how I was faint
And yet how wise I was in loving you.

XX

How much a garland pleases when it lies,
Woven with flowers, upon some golden hair;
It seems as if each blossom thrusts and tries
To be the first to kiss that forehead fair.

Contented all day long that garment is
Which spreads itself but first clings to her breast.
The golden thread asks nothing but to rest,
Touching her cheeks and throat with tenderness.

More honoured still that ribbon which can lie,
Gilded and shaped in the most cunning fashion,
Touching the breast which it so carefully laces.

And that small belt that knots so easily
Seems to declare, 'Unceasing my caresses.'
Would that my arms might join in such a passion!

XXXIV

TO TOMMASO DE CAVALIERI

Eternal fire is kindly to cold stone
And draws strength from it. And though stone may fall
To ashes, it has never really gone
But lives in fire and is not lost at all.

And if, in furnaces, through every season
It lasts, it has achieved a higher place,
Just as a purged soul moves from its own prison
And flies to heaven adorned with every grace.

It is the same with me when fierce desires
Reduce me to pale ashes, dry and cold:
I am not lost but find new life indeed.

If I can rise from ashes which seem dead
And come unscathed from these consuming fires,
I am not forged from iron but from gold.

XLVIII

Though long delay breeds greater tenderness
Than our desires in youth can ever know,
Still I regret my love's belatedness—
That passion has so short a time to go.

Heaven is perverse indeed if in its care
For us it still can set old hearts on fire.
This is the fate I must accept and bear—
To love a woman with a sad desire.

Yet may be when the sun sinks in the west
And end of day is reached, I can at least
Be in the greater dark a single shade.

If love has come to me when life must fade,
If I desire, though death must touch me soon,
Oh, of my sunset, Lady, make my noon!

LV

My Lord, you know that I know that you know
That I have come to be more close, more near.
You know that I know what is known to you,
Why then do we delay in greeting here?

If all that you have said is really true,
And if, which you admit, my trust is real,
Then break the wall dividing us, and know
A double strength can greater woes conceal.

If in you, I love only, my dear Lord,
What you love more yourself, do not be hurt
That with one soul another should accord.

That in your noble face which I love most
Is scarcely known by human mind and heart.
He who would see it must become a ghost.

LX

(1)

Sometimes hope rises strongly with desire,
And surely such a hope may not be held
As false; if heaven is angry with such fire,
Then to what end did God create the world?

What better reason can there be to love,
Than to give glory to the God on high?
He who is pleased with you dwells up above,
And every good heart he will purify.

Only false hopes can claim a love that dies.
Such love depends on beauty which grows less,
And the swift change of mortal loveliness.

Sweet is that hope which in the modest heart
Is steadfast though all surface things depart!
Such faithful love's a pledge of paradise.

LXVII

TO GIORGIO VASARI

There is no lower thing on earth than I
Conceive myself to be when I lack you.
My weak and tired spirit makes me sigh
For pardon for all things I've failed to do.

Stretch down to me, Oh God, that powerful chain
That knots all heavenly gifts. Such faith and trust
Are what I long forever to attain;
It is my fault I am not fully blest.

The more I think of faith, more rare and good
It seems, and even greater may it be
Since all the world depends on it for peace.

You never were a miser of your blood:
If Heaven is locked to every other key,
What kind of gifts of mercy, then, are these?

LXIX

TO MONSIGNOR LODOVICO BECCADELLI

My death is certain but the hour unsure,
Life is so brief and little now have I;
So sweet it is to sense, yet cannot lure
The soul. My spirit prays that I may die.

The world is bad, and evil customs still
Defeat good habits, cast good actions out.
The light's extinguished, pride and daring will
Make false things triumph, call the truth in doubt.

Oh God, when will that time arrive which he,
Who trusts in you, expects? Hope falls away,
And fatal to the soul is great delay.

What good is it that light and clarity
Should shine for others if, before it dies,
The soul is lost in such uncertainties?

LXX

Loaded with years and full of all my sins,
Rooted in habits evil and yet strong,
I feel two deaths approach me. Now begins
The heart's division, poisoned for so long.

Nor have I all the forces which I need
To change my life and love, custom and fate.
Only your grace and power can intercede
And guide our steps before it is too late.

It is not now enough, Oh Lord, that I
Wish to be made anew. I cannot be
The same as when, from nothing, you made me.

I beg you — halve that way so steep and high
Before you take my body from my soul:
And may I come back purified and whole.

LXXI

Now that I need men's pity and compassion,
And can no longer scoff and laugh at all
The faults of others, now my soul must fall
Unguided, lacking its own domination.

Only one flag can I now serve beneath,
And with it conquer life. I speak of faith.
Only with this can I face the attack
Of all my foes, when other help I lack.

Oh flesh, Oh blood, Oh wood, Oh pain extreme!
Let all my sins be purified through you
From whom I came, as did my father too.

So good you are, your pity is supreme;
Only your help can save my evil fate:
So close to death, so far from God my state.

LXXIII

Unburdened by the body's fierce demands,
And now at last released from my frail boat,
Dear God, I put myself into your hands;
Smooth the rough waves on which my ship must float.

The thorns, the nails, the wounds in both your palms,
The gentleness, the pity on your face—
For great repentance, these have promised grace.
My soul will find salvation in your arms.

And let not justice only fill your eyes,
But mercy too. Oh temper your severe
Judgment with tenderness, relieve my burden.

Let your own blood remove my faults and clear
My guilt, and let your grace so strongly rise
That I am granted an entire pardon.

LXXIV

(I)

Simply the longing for more years to live
Seems to hold out a promise. Yet I know
That death's approach is never made more slow,
That only sorrows have the power to give

A sense of halting. Yet how foolish is
A longing for more life and pleasure when
God is found best in human miseries.
The happier life, the more it hurts again.

And if, dear God, your grace assails my heart
And sets it burning with a fiery zeal,
Which deep within my spirit I can feel,

Then I from my own gifts would gladly part
And rise to Heaven at once, since I am sure
My good desires on earth will not endure.

LXXIV

(II)

Often, I think, a great desire may
Hold out the promise of more time to me.
Yet death has power to whittle me away
The more I live and breathe delightedly.

What better time for my sure transformation
Than when I pray, in grief, to God above?
Then lead me, Lord, to my true destination,
And all my earthly cares and joys remove.

For in this way your grace assails my heart
With faith and all its strong and fervent zeal.
From such a comfort I would never part.

Alone, I shall for certain always fail:
Then plant in me that faith such as you give
To angels who, without you, cannot live.

LXXV

I wish, God, for some end I do not will.
Between the fire and heart a veil of ice
Puts out the fire. My pen will not move well,
So that the sheet on which I'm working lies.

I pay you mere lip-service, then I grieve;
Love does not reach my heart, I do not know
How to admit that grace which would relieve
My state and crush the arrogance I show.

Oh tear away that veil, God, break that wall
Which with its strength refuses to let in
The sun whose light has vanished from the world.

Send down the promised light to bless and hold
Your lovely bride. So may I seek for all
I need in you, both end there and begin.

LXXVI

Those souls for whom you died were sad as well
As happy that you chose death for their sake.
The blood you shed had locked the doors of Hell,
And opened Heaven for all mankind to take.

Happy they were because you had redeemed
Man from his first mistake and final loss.
But they were sad such suffering had claimed
Your flesh which died for all men on the cross.

Heaven gave a sign that she had seen it all;
Her eyes grew dim, the earth beneath her showed
A gulf, the waters rushed, the mountains shook.

Christ snatched the Fathers from their dark abode
But sent the devils to a greater fall;
All baptised men for his own joy he took.

LXXVII

Although it saddens me and causes pain,
The past, which is not with me any more,
Brings me relief, since all that I abhor—
My sin and guilt—will not come back again.

Precious it is to me because I learn,
Before death comes, how brief is happiness:
But sad also, since when at last I turn
For pardon, grace may yet refuse to bless.

Although, Oh God, your promise I attend,
It is too much to ask you to forgive
Those who for pardon have so long delayed.

But in the blood you shed, I understand
What recompense and mercy you've displayed,
Showering your precious gifts that we may live.

LXXVIII

Dear to me is sleep: still more, being made of stone.
While pain and guilt still linger here below,
Blindness and numbness — these please me alone;
Then do not wake me, keep your voices low.

NEW POEMS

FOR LOVE

I did not know the names of love
And now they have grown few.
When I this way or that behave,
I want the meaning too.
I want the definition when
The feeling starts to go.

'Yes now,' 'Yes now', or 'It has come' —
Lovers have used these names;
But each one thinks he has found some-
thing separate and strange.
In all the lonely darknesses
We think a new truth gleams.

I am worn out with thinking of
The feelings I have had.
Some strange hand seems to grasp my love
And pull it from the bed.
I wait for clear, undreaming nights
And letters now instead.

THE CIRCLE

The circle closes
And we are locked in it.
It is complete, it impinges
Only on what it knows, it
Stays always the same size, only
We (cowering in the centre)
Swell and shrink,
Love or are afraid.

All our known worlds
We make circular. They
Complete us. Round
Or flat does not matter.
They are our idea of safety
And of eternity.
It seems then that,
Of all our aphorisms,
This one is true—
The endless is our home.

THE SHAKING WORLD

Under all this
There is violence.
The chairs, tables, pictures, paper-weights
Are all moving, moving.
You can't see it but they are being carried
Along with currents and continents.
We too are carried (our peace two quarrelling doves)
And nothing, nothing is still.

A Buddhist monk at his most uplifted
High in the Himalayas
Is moved too.
Great wheels of the world bear him round and round.
We have tried to tie the universe to horoscopes
While we whirl between star and star.

A DREAM OF BIRTH

It was a coming out to newness,
It was a hatching, a breaking,
I stretched my limbs finally and they came, came.
Newmade, I could feel my own pulse
And the shell around me dissolved, I let it go,
And then I began to feel green things and grow.

A pulse was under my fingers, a baby's, a child's pleasure,
Also a marriage rite was being performed.
I took part in it gently, gently.
In the spine of pleasure, a power was rising, rising.
I watched and the world was warmed.

THE UNKNOWN CHILD

That child will never lie in me, and you
Will never be its father. Mirrors must
Replace the real image, make it true
So that the gentle love-making we do
Has powerful passions and a parents' trust.

That child will never lie in me and make
Our loving careful. We must kiss and touch
Quietly and watch our own reflexions break
As in a pool that is disturbed. Oh take
My watchful love; there must not be too much

A child lies within my mind. I see
The eyes, the hands. I see you also there,
I see you waiting with an honest care,
Within my mind, within me bodily,
And birth and death close to us constantly.

THE BOY

The pulse
Of the city
Beats loud.
He waits,
Leans against shop-door, on gates,
Watches people boldly, puts
His hand in his belt, feels proud
Of his face and genitals.

The crowd
Moves past
Like low thunder.
Girls too move past.
He is like a young bull under
Some self-chosen yoke.
He will move soon.
An invisible matador will brandish his cloak,
And a girl will throw down a red flower
In the middle of the wide afternoon.

THE OPERATION

The operation is over now.
He lies in clean linen, hands stretched out.
He is asleep still, mercifully.
When he arouses, the pain will be harsh.

Where is he now, in what limbo?
What kind creatures hover over him?
What dark beasts terrify him?
The world is hushed to a kind of death.
There is the smell of ether and medicines.

A few huge flowers bow beside him;
They breathe scent, they mean life,
Someone thrust them in his vase.
They speak, mutely, of life and creation
And go on speaking as their petals fall.

THE NOVICE

She turns her head demurely. In a year
Or two she will
Be able to smile openly at all.
She once enjoyed so much. Now there's a wall,
Also a grille.
Only the narrow, indoor things are clear.

She is not certain yet if she will stay.
She watches those
Who have been living here for many years.
No doubt upon each timeless face appears.
These stayed and chose
And in their suffering learnt how to pray.

Upon her window-sill two turtle doves
Gently demur.
All of the noisy world is here brought low
To these quiet birds who come and go
And seem to her
So far removed from all she hates and loves.

SHOCK

Seeing you cry
Is, for me,
Like seeing others die.

You have been changeless, permanent
As the Equator,
Equal to all tides and suns.
Now it is as if you were a volcano
With a shattered crater.

It is elemental — this.
It is like plants budding, animals mating.
There would be fires and stars in a swift kiss,
Your tears are a storm starting.

THE BONFIRE

It is burning the winter away.
The smoke is coming like clouds over sea,
It has its own tides,
Its own laws.
There are only small flowers to see:
Nothing like fireworks or stars.

But it is a herald,
An augury.
These tight buds of flame
Will burst later on borders and flower-beds
Most decorously.

All passion is like this—
Like the spent rose
Veering and turning in a bevy of winds
Till the seed overflows.

VOLCANO AND ICEBERG

There will be an explosion one day,
This calm exterior will crack,
Seas will come up,
New islands,
New devastations.
This is me, this is me.

Sail round me, yachts, smacks, steamers,
Explorers come nearer,
Seven-eighths of me is below the surface.
One day, soon, that seven-eighths is coming to the top.

So beautiful I am
With my calm face
But I am cold to the touch,
I can also burn you,
I am saying something about stars and climates.
Soon the explosion is coming.
I don't want to be there then.

GALE

There is an inland gale
And I dream of sea-winds and lobsters.
My mind is open to the full
Places, the islands and harbours:

Also to the lonely ones
The far-off wave
Topped by a bird long-since,
Seeming to speak of love.

And of Noah's Ark I dream —
The gentle animals
Two by two still come —
I hear their footfalls.

And last of all the salt
Taste of the sea and spring
So far inland is felt
Stranger than anything.

INDEX OF FIRST LINES